CREATIONISM IN TWENTIETH-CENTURY AMERICA

Volume 3

THE ANTIEVOLUTION WORKS OF ARTHUR I. BROWN

THE ANTIEVOLUTION WORKS OF ARTHUR I. BROWN

Edited by
RONALD L. NUMBERS

LONDON AND NEW YORK

First published in 1995 by Garland Publishing, Inc.

This edition first published in 2022
by Routledge
4 Park Square, Milton Park, Abingdon, Oxon OX14 4RN
605 Third Avenue, New York, NY 10017

Routledge is an imprint of the Taylor & Francis Group, an informa business

© 1995 Introductions Copyright Ronald L. Numbers

All rights reserved. No part of this book may be reprinted or reproduced or utilised in any form or by any electronic, mechanical, or other means, now known or hereafter invented, including photocopying and recording, or in any information storage or retrieval system, without permission in writing from the publishers.

Trademark notice: Product or corporate names may be trademarks or registered trademarks, and are used only for identification and explanation without intent to infringe.

British Library Cataloguing in Publication Data
A catalogue record for this book is available from the British Library

ISBN: 978-0-367-43553-0 (Set)
ISBN: 978-1-00-314991-0 (Set) (ebk)
ISBN: 978-0-367-41498-6 (Volume 3) (hbk)
ISBN: 978-0-367-41500-6 (Volume 3) (pbk)
ISBN: 978-0-367-81486-1 (Volume 3) (ebk)

DOI: 10.4324/9780367814861

Publisher's Note
The publisher has gone to great lengths to ensure the quality of this reprint but points out that some imperfections in the original copies may be apparent.

Disclaimer
The publisher has made every effort to trace copyright holders and would welcome correspondence from those they have been unable to trace.

New Preface to the Re-issue of 2021

This anthology of primary documents related to the early history of creationism in the United States first appeared a quarter century ago, in 1995. My interest in the topic had been aroused by my years of research on creationism, which resulted in *The Creationists* (New York: Alfred A. Knopf, 1992). In the meantime, a former student of mine, Edward J. Larson, had published an excellent legal survey, *Trial and Error: The American Controversy over Creation and Evolution* (New York: Oxford University Press, 1985). The philosopher of science Michael Ruse had published the edited volume *But Is It Science? The Philosophical Question in the Creation/Evolution Controversy* (Amherst, NY: Prometheus Books, 1988); and the anthropologist Christopher P. Toumey had just released *God's Own Scientists: Creationists in a Secular World* (New Brunswick, NJ: Rutgers University Press, 1994). Led by Willard B. Gatewood's *Preachers Pedagogues and Politicians: The Evolution Controversy in North Carolina, 1920–1927* (Chapel Hill: University of North Carolina Press, 1966), local studies had also begun to appear. Nevertheless, few, if any, research libraries had begun collecting creationist literature; and not one, to my knowledge, possessed even a complete run of the *Creation Research Society Quarterly*, launched in 1964.

During the past quarter century the landscape of creationism has changed dramatically. Since 1995 the institutional heart of creationism has shifted from the Institute for Creation Research, founded by Henry M. Morris in southern California in 1972, to Ken Ham's Answers in Genesis, headquartered in northern Kentucky. In 2007 the charismatic Australian-born Ham opened a $27-million Creation Museum in Petersburg, Kentucky, across the Ohio River from Cincinnati. Forty-five miles away, in Williamstown, Kentucky, Ham in July 2016 opened an Ark Encounter featuring a "life-size" replica of Noah's ark, at a projected cost of $150 million.

Such growth has attracted considerable attention, such as Susan L. Trollinger and William Vance Trollinger Jr., *Righting America at the Creation Museum* (Baltimore: Johns Hopkins University Press, 2016), and James S. Bielo, *Ark Encounter: The Making of a Creationist Theme Park* (New York: New York University Press, 2018).

The literature on the general history of creationism in the twentieth century has exploded, symbolized most dramatically by Edward J. Larson's Pulitzer Prize-winning volume *Summer for the Gods: The Scopes Trial and America's Continuing Debate over Science and Religion* (New York: Basic Books, 1997). Other significant contributions include Michael Lienesch, *In the Beginning: Fundamentalism, the Scopes Trial, and the Making of the Antievolution Movement* (Chapel Hill: University of North Carolina, 2007); Adam Laats, *Fundamentalism and Education in the Scopes Era: God, Darwin, and the Roots of America's Culture Wars* (New York: Palgrave Macmillan, 2010); Jeffrey P. Moran, *American Genesis: The Evolution Controversies from Scopes to Creation Science* (New York: Oxford University Press, 2012); and Adam R. Shapiro, *Trying Biology: The Scopes Trial, Textbooks, and the Antievolution Movement in American Schools* (Chicago: University of Chicago Press, 2013).

Still, access to creationist sources before the early 1960s remains patchy. To help remedy this condition, Routledge has agreed to reissue the 10-volume set of *Creationism in Twentieth-Century America*. I thank them for their continuing interest.

Ronald L. Numbers
April 2021

CREATIONISM IN TWENTIETH-CENTURY AMERICA

A Ten-Volume Anthology of Documents, 1903–1961

Series Editor
RONALD L. NUMBERS
University of Wisconsin–Madison
William Coleman Professor of the
History of Science and Medicine

Series Contents

1. ANTIEVOLUTIONISM BEFORE WORLD WAR I

2. CREATION-EVOLUTION DEBATES

3. THE ANTIEVOLUTION WORKS OF ARTHUR I. BROWN

4. THE ANTIEVOLUTION PAMPHLETS OF WILLIAM BELL RILEY

5. THE CREATIONIST WRITINGS OF BYRON C. NELSON

6. THE ANTIEVOLUTION PAMPHLETS OF HARRY RIMMER

7. SELECTED WORKS OF GEORGE McCREADY PRICE

8. THE EARLY WRITINGS OF HAROLD W. CLARK AND FRANK LEWIS MARSH

9. EARLY CREATIONIST JOURNALS

10. CREATION AND EVOLUTION IN THE EARLY AMERICAN SCIENTIFIC AFFILIATION

VOLUME 3

THE ANTIEVOLUTION WORKS OF ARTHUR I. BROWN

Edited with introductions by
RONALD L. NUMBERS
*University of Wisconsin—Madison
William Coleman Professor of the
History of Science and Medicine*

First published by Garland Publishing, Inc.

This edition published 2011 by Routledge:

Routledge
Taylor & Francis Group
711 Third Avenue
New York, NY 10017

Routledge
Taylor & Francis Group
2 Park Square, Milton Park
Abingdon, Oxon OX14 4RN

Introductions copyright © 1995 Ronald L. Numbers
All rights reserved

Library of Congress Cataloging-in-Publication Data

Brown, Arthur I., 1875–1947.
   The antievolution works of Arthur I. Brown / edited with introductions by Ronald L. Numbers.
      p.   cm. — (Creationism in twentieth-century America ; v. 3)
   Includes bibliographical references.
   ISBN 0-8153-1804-9 (alk. paper)
   1. Creationism. 2. Bible and evolution. 3. Evolution—Religious aspects—Christianity. 4. Evolution—Controversial literature. 5. Evolution (Biology)—Religious aspects—Christianity.   I. Numbers, Ronald L. II. Title. III. Series.
BS651.B7874   1995
231—dc20   94-45075
                                                                                CIP

Contents

Series Introduction	vii
Volume Introduction	ix
Evolution and the Bible	1
Evolution and the Blood-Precipitation Test	29
God's Creative Forethought	61
Men, Monkeys and Missing Links	97
Science Speaks to Osborn	129
Was Darwin Right?	159
Acknowledgments	209

Series Introduction

In recent years creationism has enjoyed a stunning renaissance both in the United States and around the world. Public opinion polls show that 47 percent of Americans, including one quarter of college graduates, believe that "God created man pretty much in his present form at one time within the last 10,000 years." In the early 1980s two states, Arkansas and Louisiana, passed laws mandating the teaching of "creation science" whenever "evolution science" was taught in the public schools. The United States Supreme Court subsequently overturned these laws, but creationists actively—and often successfully—continue to promote their cause in local schools and churches.

Since the early 1960s creationism has become increasingly identified with a particular nonevolutionary belief known as "scientific creationism" or "creation science." Scientific creationists believe that all life on earth originated no more than 10,000 years ago, and some argue that the entire universe is equally young. To explain the appearance of age suggested by the fossil record, they typically invoke Noah's flood, which, they claim, deposited virtually the entire geological column in the span of a year or so.

Before the 1960s relatively few Americans, including religious fundamentalists, subscribed to such restrictive views of earth history. At the height of the antievolution controversies of the 1920s, for example, most creationists who expressed themselves on the subject embraced interpretations of the book of Genesis that allowed them to accept the evidence of historical geology for the antiquity of life on earth. They generally did so in one of two ways: either by assuming that the "days" of Genesis 1 really meant "ages" or by interposing a gap of perhaps hundreds of millions of years between the creation "in the beginning" and the relatively recent Edenic creation (or restoration, as some would call it) associated with Adam and Eve. Only a few fundamentalists at the time, mostly Seventh-day Adventists, insisted on the recent appearance of life and on the geological significance of the deluge. In recent years, however, through the influence of books such as John C. Whitcomb, Jr. and Henry M. Morris's *The Genesis Flood* (1961), organizations such as the Creation Research Society (1963) and institutions such as the Institute for Creation Research (1972), the so-called flood geologists, now known as scientific creationists, have co-opted the very name creationist for their once peculiar views.

Despite the undeniable importance of antievolutionism in American cultural history, few libraries, academic or otherwise, have collected more than the odd book or pamphlet on creationism, and early creationist periodicals are almost impossible to find. Whether the result of prejudice or indifference, such neglect has made it difficult for students and scholars to explore the development of creationist thought in the twentieth century. This collection of reprinted documents from the first six decades of the century makes available some of the most widely read works on creationism by such stalwarts as Arthur I. Brown, William Bell Riley, Harry Rimmer, Byron C. Nelson, George McCready Price, Harold W. Clark, and Frank Lewis Marsh. It also reprints, for the first time, three of the earliest and rarest creationist journals in America: the *Creationist*, the *Bulletin of Deluge Geology*, and the *Forum for the Correlation of Science and the Bible*.

INTRODUCTION

In 1926 antievolutionists in North Carolina hyperbolically hailed the visiting lecturer Arthur I. Brown, M.D., C.M., F.R.C.S.E., as the "greatest scientist in all the world." The doctor's own handbills more modestly introduced him as "one of the best informed scientists on the American continent." Whatever his reputation in the wider world of science, during the 1920s and 1930s Brown undoubtedly ranked among the top three or four scientific critics of evolution in the fundamentalist community.[1]

Brown, though born in the United States in 1875, called Vancouver, British Columbia, his home. He received his M.D. from Trinity Medical College, Toronto, in 1897 and became a fellow of the Royal College of Surgeons of Edinburgh in 1913, having completed "a very stiff post graduate course taken in Scotland." (The C.M. after his name stood for a British master of surgery degree.) Apparently later that same year he began practicing surgery in Vancouver, eventually becoming, in his own estimation, "one of the leading surgeons of the Pacific Coast" and earning a reported (and perhaps exaggerated) $50,000 a year at a time when most physicians in North America still made less than one-tenth that amount.[2]

Little is known about Brown's spiritual and intellectual development, but by the early 1920s he was publishing antievolution pamphlets on such subjects as *Evolution and the Bible* (1922) and *Men, Monkeys and Missing Links* (1923). Despite his superior knowledge of science, at least for a creationist, he contributed few novel ideas to the cause; instead, he tended to popularize the works of others and to use illustrations of apparent design in the natural world to argue for the necessity of special creation. In *Men, Monkeys and Missing Links*, for example, he provided a synopsis of *God—or Gorilla* (1922), a sneering, indignant attack on human evolution by a muckraking Catholic journalist, Alfred Watterson McCann (1879–1931), who reveled in exposing Piltdown man as a hoax years before the scientific community conceded that it was. Although McCann had no sympathy for fundamentalism, Brown lauded his book as a "great work" that offered "the most scathing and unanswerable indictment ever published against this untenable hypothesis." Perhaps Brown's original contribution to the arsenal of antievolution polemics was a critique of arguments for evolution based on laboratory analyses of blood serum from animals and humans, which provided scientists with a means of identifying lines of descent that turned out to be identical to those suggested by morphological studies. In *Evolution and the Blood-Precipitation Test* (1925) Brown argued that biologists had no justification for assuming that animals having chemically similar blood shared a common ancestor, because similarities in blood types could also be explained by appealing to "an Omniscient and Omnipotent Creator and Designer."[3]

Brown claimed to reject evolution because it seemed "contrary to the clear facts of Science as well as to the plain statements of Scripture," which he believed to be "infallible and inerrant from Gen. 1:1 to Rev. 22:21." In his opinion evolution was not only "the greatest hoax ever foisted on a credulous world" but also "the most potent and effective weapon which is being used by Satan in his present furious attack on the Bible." However, like most fundamentalists during the first half of the century, he had no quarrel with evidence for an ancient earth, believing that the language of Genesis 1 allowed for the passage of "unknown ages" between the original creation "in the beginning" and the subsequent Edenic restoration. On the basis of an obscure passage in Ezekiel 28:17, he surmised that the first creation had been wiped out by a stupendous catastrophe, possibly a flood, caused by the "Devil's hatred of God when he was thrown or 'cast' to the ground." But although he assiduously sought to decipher biblical prophecies that seemed to foretell the imminent return of Christ and had no doubt that the "days" of creation were twenty-four hours in length, for the most part he avoided discussions of the exact meaning of the first chapters of Genesis.[4]

In November 1925, "at the urgent solicitation of many prominent Fundamentalist leaders," Brown took a one-year leave of absence from his lucrative surgical practice in order to devote his time to lecturing on science and the Bible. The demand for his services proved so great he gave up medicine permanently and lived off the contributions received during his lectures, frequently delivered in large Baptist churches. His life-style seems to have suffered little as a result of this decision; he did well enough financially to travel with his wife, stay in the finest hotels, and hire an advance man. For years he maintained a grueling pace, crisscrossing the country to meet engagements. Early in 1929, for example, he wrote from upstate New York about the "wonderful series of campaigns here in the East, Philadelphia, New York,

Boston, Paterson, Passaic, Camden, Brooklyn, Atlantic City, Baltimore, Washington, and now am at First Baptist Church here in Buffalo." From Buffalo and Rochester he planned to head west to Cleveland, Pontiac, Racine, Chicago, Springfield, St. Louis, and Kansas City. After more than three years on the road, he showed no signs of burning out. "Crowds everywhere, intense interest, and invariable requests for return engagements," he proudly reported to a preacher in Forth Worth whom he would soon be visiting. "I can promise you audiences will be clamoring for more when I have finished."[5]

Brown's appeal, which even he and his wife professed to find surprising, stemmed more from his reputation as a world-famous scientist than from his platform manner. Given his alleged credentials, explained one newspaper reporter, audiences expected that "at the blast of his ram's horn the walled city of modern knowledge was to tumble." Even fundamentalists who generally had little use for the trappings of higher education took pride in his professional accomplishments, mistaking them for academic achievement. "Notice the degrees attached to the writer's name," wrote one Kansas editor in introducing an antievolution piece by Brown, "realize that he was trained in some of the best Universities in Europe, and you will know why he is recognized as an authority." The president of Wheaton College in Illinois, eager to improve the academic standing and visibility of his fundamentalist institution, coveted the services of the creationist savant, and virtually every antievolution organization sought the use of his name. The Bible Crusaders of America, founded by the Boston capitalist George F. Washburn (1859–1931), honored him with the title Scientist General.[6]

Unlike some of the fire-and-brimstone preachers who damned evolution, Brown shunned pyrotechnics. A far-from-partisan reporter covering his 1926 campaign in Raleigh, North Carolina, observed that the visiting celebrity, who had "quit medical doctoring for divinity doseing [sic]," possessed "a great deal more sense, scholarship, personality and platform ability than most of the agitators" who sought to outlaw the teaching of Darwinism. Although the reporter thought Brown's "scientific speech" fell dead, he applauded the lecturer's gentleness and civility. Years later a graduate student at the University of Minnesota who met Brown during a crusade in Minneapolis found the itinerant surgeon to be "perhaps the most godly, gracious Christian gentleman I ever met, as well as one of the finest Bible teachers and creationist scientists." Brown was not, however, above directing some occasional humor at evolutionists. In "'Bunk' and the 'Monk,'" a poem lampooning the efforts of scientists to explain evolution, he concluded with the following verse:

> So, we're cousins to moles, to fish and tadpoles,
> Don't smile friends, beware,—that's called "science" today,
> We've a "common ancestor"—You've heard of the quest, sir
> His old bones they do hunt night and day.
> But though hot on the trail of this mythical tail
> There's no trace, of poor lost chimpanzee.
> And this "brain-stormy" theory can't answer my query,—
> Not one ape roosts in my family tree!

Brown's ministry ended prematurely when he died in an automobile accident late in 1947.[7]

NOTES

This introduction is taken from Ronald L. Numbers, *The Creationists* (New York: Alfred A. Knopf, 1992), pp. 57–60, and is reprinted with the permission of the publisher.

1. Handbill advertising Brown's lectures at the First Baptist Church, Buffalo, December 30, 1928–January 6, 1929, J. Frank Norris Collection, Dargan-Carver Library of the Historical Commission of the Southern Baptist Convention, Nashville, Tennessee; see also *Greensboro Daily News*, May 17, 1926, from a clipping in fld. 310, William Louis Poteat Papers, Baptist Historical Collection, Wake Forest University Library.

2. Information about Brown's training comes from various editions of the *American Medical Directory* and from the Trinity College Archives. See also Willard B. Gatewood, Jr., ed., *Controversy in the Twenties: Fundamentalism, Modernism, and Evolution* (Nashville: Vanderbilt University Press, 1969), p. 154 (American birth); J. Oliver Buswell, Jr., to S.J. Bole, May 1, 1928, Bole's personnel file, Wheaton College (postgraduate course); and the editor's introduction to Arthur I. Brown, "Darwin and Sir Arthur Keith," *Defender* 2 (November 1927): 3 (salary). On the income of physicians in early twentieth-century Vancouver, see Margaret W. Andrews, "Medical Attendance in Vancouver, 1886–1920," *Medicine in Canadian Society: Historical Perspectives*, ed. S. E. D. Shortt (Montreal: McGill-Queen's University Press, 1981), pp. 416–45.

3. Arthur I. Brown, *Evolution and the Bible* (Vancouver, BC: Arcade Printers, [1922]); Brown, *Men, Monkeys and Missing Links* (Vancouver, BC: n.p., 1923), quotation on p. 3; Brown, *Evolution and the Blood-*

Precipitation Test (Los Angeles: Research Science Bureau, [1925]), quotation on p. 30. See also Brown, *Footprints of God* (Findlay, OH: Dunham Publishing, 1943); Brown, *Miracles of Science* (Findlay, OH: Dunham Publishing, 1945); Brown, *God's Creative Forethought* (Findlay, OH: Fundamental Truth Publishers, n.d.); and Brown, *God and You: Wonders of the Human Body* (Findlay, OH: Fundamental Truth Publishers, n.d.). Regarding McCann, see Alfred Watterson McCann, *God—or Gorilla: How the Monkey Theory of Evolution Exposes Its Own Methods, Refutes Its Own Principles, Denies Its Own Inferences, Disproves Its Own Case* (New York: Devin-Adair, 1922).

4 Brown, *God and You*, pp. 8–9 (infallible); Brown, *Footprints of God*, pp. 24 (hoax), 135 (unknown ages); Brown, *Was Darwin Right?* (Glendale, CA: Glendale News, n.d.), p. 49 (weapon). Typical of Brown's prophetic writings is *I Will Come Again* (Findlay, OH: Fundamental Truth Publishers, 1947). On his belief in literal days, see the *Greensboro Daily News*, May 17, 1926, from a clipping in fld. 310, Poteat Papers.

5 A.I. Brown to Frank Norris, January 4, 1929, and handbill advertising Brown's lectures at the First Baptist Church, Buffalo, both in the Norris Collection.

6 *Greensboro Daily News*, May 17, 1926, from a clipping in fld., 310, Poteat Papers; Gerald B. Winrod's introduction to Arthur I. Brown, "'Vestigal Organs,'" *Defender* 1 (June 1926): 6; J.O. Buswell to S.J. Bole, May 1, 1928; Stewart G. Cole, *The History of Fundamentalism* (New York: Richard R. Smith, 1931), p. 272 (Scientist General).

7 *Greensboro Daily News*, May 16 and 17, 1926, from clippings in fld. 310, Poteat Papers; Henry M. Morris, *A History of Modern Creationism* (San Diego: Master Book Publishers, 1984), pp. 101–03; *The Crusaders' Champion* 1 (December 25, 1925): 18, quoted in Gatewood, *Controversy in the Twenties*, pp. 405–07. On Brown's lectures in Paducah, Kentucky, and Tucson, Arizona, see, respectively, Maynard Shipley, *The War on Modern Science: A Short History of the Fundamentalist Attacks on Evolution and Modernism* (New York: Alfred A. Knopf, 1927), pp. 123–24, and George E. Webb, "Tucson's Evolution Debate, 1924–1927," *Journal of Arizona History* 24 (1983): 6–7. See also "Dr. A.I. Brown of Vancouver Dies in Crash" (Victoria) *Daily Colonist*, November 4, 1947, p. 2.

EVOLUTION AND THE BIBLE

BY
ARTHUR I. BROWN, M.D., C.M., F.R.C.S.E.
VANCOUVER, B. C.

PRICE TEN CENTS

VANCOUVER:
THE ARCADE PRINTERS
365 Cordova Street

FOREWORD

By the REV. W. ELLIS, M.A., B.D.
Principal of the Vancouver Bible Training School

We live in days when it is unpopular to accept anything on faith, or to explain things in any other way than in terms of some law. Psychology has sought to explain the phenomena connected with the mind—even to the matter of conversion—according to well defined laws. It is sometimes said that "spiritual healing" can be practised by anyone who knows the laws governing it, and that the so-called miracles of Christ were wrought by Him because He had perfect understanding.

There is a grave possibility of overdoing this reign of natural law. The law may be so exalted that the Law-giver is ousted from His throne. This is notably the case in the matter of Evolution. We even hear of "the law of evolution." There is much danger of corrupting and even demolishing faith in our Lord Jesus Christ, and His divine authority, as well as the authority of the Scriptures, from the assumption of this law of evolution. I say "assumption" advisedly, and the men who are our leading scientists do not recognize a "law of evolution." It is, with them, only an hypothesis, a supposition. At the meeting of the British Association for the Advancement of Science in Edinburgh last year, Dr. D. H. Scott, the President of the Botany section, said that the theory of evolution was held as "an act of faith," and that "for the moment, at all events, the Darwinian period is past."

It is unfortunate for the cause of truth that there is such a wide-spread, but unjustified assumption of the "law" of evolution, but the pamphlet of my friend Dr. A. I. Brown has "come to the kingdom for such a time as this." The thoughtful and open-minded reader of this pamphlet will see quite clearly that there are some insuperable difficulties to the acceptance of evolution, from the scientific, logical and spiritual sides. I hope and pray that it may have a very wide circulation because I am confident that it will result in bringing glory to Him "by Whom all things were made."

EVOLUTION AND THE BIBLE

FOR the past two decades the world has been literally drenched with a veritable flood of writings and addresses by men, known and unknown,—mostly the latter—who have made agonizing attempts either to show that Science and the Bible are hopelessly at variance, or that they may, after certain mental adjustments, be brought into accord with one another.

Those chiefly concerned in this attempt are certain scientists with an anti-Christian bias, and a class of preachers, the latter impressed by the bogey of a false but blatant scholarship. They have sought to prove that wherever the Bible touches a scientific question, the author wrote simply as a man, expressing his own scientific knowledge, which was not more than that of the time in which he lived. Hence it is explained that we must expect grave errors in the scientific statements of the Scriptures. We are asked to remember that the Bible was not intended to teach scientific, but spiritual truths. When we find what we think are mistakes, we need not be disturbed, because they are not God's views, but man's.

In other words, these fallible human authors had infallible insight into things spiritual, which one would think are just as difficult of discernment as things scientific, but when they wrote of the less important matters like the origin of matter, life, man, and the universe in general, they lost the power to speak truth. The God who spoke through them the most sublime and uplifting spiritual truths, did not consider it worth while to direct their thoughts and words when they wrote about the physical realm. On the contrary, He allowed them to speak as erring and ignorant humans, uttering only the imperfect and childish views of their ancient day. Thus the story of Creation becomes nothing more than an interesting collection of nursery yarns.

And yet we are asked to believe that God used their errors and childish poetical fables to reveal through them the most wonderful truths to a seeking but sinning world. Surely this must be the first and only instance of a structure of righteousness and truth founded on superstition and falsehood!

the Jewish people among whom He lived, and with whom He claimed relationship?

TWO HORNS OF THE DILEMMA

It must be one or the other. In the first case, He is guilty of deceiving His followers, when by a word He could have revealed the truth to them, and saved them, and all succeeding generations, from gross error. In the second case, we worship a fallible, human Saviour, not God, made flesh, revealing Omnipotence and Omniscience to a fallen race.

In both cases, the foundations of Christianity are undermined, and our religion is built on shifting quicksand, not on solid rock, on error, not on truth, and, as so many professed followers are now doing, we may as well abandon it.

THE MYTH OF A CARELESS GOD

In view of the sinless perfection of Christ's life, and of His essential Deity, of which we have ample and convincing proof, and accepting the fact of His omnipotent power to control any instrument He might use, we refuse to believe that He would permit glaring errors like these to be written down by His human scribes.

WHITHER ARE WE BEING LED AND WHY?

We do not take an extreme view of the situation as it exists to-day. There is no alternative left to the thinking man or woman. We are not to be side-tracked from a consideration of the obvious result of the acceptance of the theory of evolution by specious and plausible arguments as to the accuracy of modern scholarship, whose exponents we are asked to follow in their devious intellectual maze, as they attempt to discredit what they are pleased to call an old-fashioned belief in the Bible.

Why, in God's name, should we forsake a Book which has never been proved in error, and has withstood thousands of hostile attacks? Why should we be expected to believe the uncertain and ever changing theories of non-Christian scientists?

It is certainly not possible to believe in the gradual evolution of man from lower forms of life, without repudiating the literal truth of Genesis, and explaining it away as myth and allegory.

THE REAL ISSUE

We are told that evolution glorifies God as much as the method of sudden Creation, mentioned in the first Book of the Bible. That is not the question at all. If God had chosen evolution as His means of peopling the earth with humanity, developing them through countless millions of years, from the primordial protoplasm in which He implanted this marvellous power of change and variation, we surely would have no right to cavil at it. The fact which is constantly overlooked is this: The Bible, supposed to be the Word of God, states that another method than evolution was used by the Creator. The issue is not between evolution and Creation, as to which brings the greater honor to God. It is between a man-made hypothesis unproven by evidence, and a simple, God-given record, supported by every known scientific discovery, which satisfies the reason of every believer in an omnipotent God.

GOD'S WISDOM AND MAN'S REASON

Of course, God is honored by **any** method which He might use to bring man and beast to full perfection, but when God's Book tells us that He did it in one particular way, what right have we to question His wisdom? What authority have we to substitute another method, even though the latter appeals to our reason? Reason is a variable quantity in every individual, and is always a poor guide. Following its lead does not always take us in the direction of truth. "The wisdom of this world is foolishness with God," and "He that sitteth in the heavens shall laugh" at the pitiful attempts of man to teach the Creator a better method than the only one the Bible mentions. And yet the man or woman who believes Genesis literally has abandoned neither logic nor common-sense. On the other hand, **Creation is infinitely more reasonable than evolution.**

THE VERACITY OF MOSES

Surely, if we say that the Mosaic record is as "near truth as the writer knew," and endeavor at the same time to convince ourselves that it is the most outstanding example in all literature, of pure and sublime inspiration, as one preacher has recently said, is to admit that ALL inspiration is nothing more than an imperfect, occasional, and very limited control, over what we have regarded as God's revelation to man of His purposes and plans for the race.

In the absence of any rational explanation, the critics kindly allow God to possess the power of creating the primal germs of life. Yet since these primal germs must have contained the potentialities of all subsequent developments, God must have possessed the power to create perfect plants and animals had He so wished. One would seem as easy as the other to an Omnipotent Creator. If He had this power, then He should possess the ability to give a clear and perfect Revelation to the world. Is it reasonable to believe that He would allow a record to bear His name and mark which does not mean what it says about an important subject like creation? Is it likely that He would give us the privilege of quarrelling over what parts we may accept, and what we may reject.

BIBLE HISTORY—TRUE OR FALSE?

If that portion of it which obviously claims to be a reliable, historical account, is not true to fact, then ALL its history may be discarded, and it follows that a Book which is not historically accurate is not spiritually true. Therefore, it cannot come from a God of righteousness and truth, and loses any possible claim on our lives.

THE MASTER HAND OF SATAN

This is always the result of persistent rejection of its literal and verbal inspiration. If there be a Devil who is opposing God's plans for the world, it would appear that his masterstroke has been reserved until the close of the campaign, and that he expects greater results from the wounding of Christianity and the Bible by professed friends, than by the attacks of avowed enemies. If he can instil doubt as to any part of the Book, and use the exponents of the Gospel as his agents, what more subtle and effective means could he employ to foster the unbelief of a godless world, and undermine the faith of those who have professed loyalty to a divinely inspired Scripture?

A QUESTION FROM THE PEW TO THE PREACHER—AN UNSOLVED PUZZLE

One finds it difficult to understand how men, calling themselves ministers of Christ, using the Bible as their Text-book, can deny portions of that upon the whole of which Christ placed His imprimatur. Consistency demands their retirement from the pulpit, or else that they should cease to use a Bible which they have virtually discarded.

EVOLUTION THE FIRST STEP TOWARDS A DISCARDED BIBLE

Undoubtedly a belief in evolution lies at the bottom of most of the modern destructive criticism of the Bible. In spite of the fact that the arguments in its favor have been shattered times without number by recent discoveries, its followers still persist in their statement that evolution has passed from the realm of theory to that of fact.

THE THEORY AND ITS ARGUMENTS

Let us examine a few of the arguments, and see if the case of the evolutionist stands the test. Only some of the most important points which are constantly emphasized will be considered, and the survey of these must necessarily be a cursory one.

EVOLUTION AND THE BIBLE

Let it be said that the anti-evolutionist is not governed in his opinion by a blind and credulous faith, but that he has facts and reason on his side. The logic of the orthodox belief is unanswerable. The opposite is so often stated that many people have come to think that those who take Genesis to mean just what it says, do so because they overlook the obvious evidence which is said to flatly contradict Creation.

Prof. J. LeConte of the University of California, defines evolution as "continuous, progressive change, according to certain laws and by means of resident forces." Many differing views are held by various schools, but all of them agree that no matter how the first primordial cell, possessing life, appeared, it was of the simplest form, and by the action of the above-mentioned progressive changes, operating through millions of years, eventually the original protoplasmic cell passed through the stages of plant, worm, fish, reptile, bird, mammal, ape, to man, to mention only a few of the different species in the long continued process.

UNIFORMITY

There are a few essential ideas connected with the theory that ought to be remembered. One is, that lying at the basis of evolution, is the idea of "Uniformity," the changes being gradual, uniform, and progressive, and we are told that the forces that operated in the beginning to bring about these changes are with us today.

It must not be forgotten that all the theories of evolution whether theistic, in which God creates the first cell, and intervenes at other stages, or atheistic, in which a Creator is excluded, are nothing more than hypotheses.

Now, if this uniform force is working today, we ought to see some of its results, that is, some species ought to be changing into other and entirely different species. But never a sign of such a thing can we discover.

EVOLUTION—NOTHING MORE THAN A THEORY—NOT A FACT

Repeating the statement that evolution is but a theory, we yet constantly hear of some preachers and professors dogmatically asserting that it is not a theory but a fact. The declarations of the small fry are often characterised by an air of cocksureness which is conspicuously lacking in the writings and addresses of the leaders in science.

Prof. H. W. Conn, in his "Evolution Today" says, "Nothing has been positively proved as to the question at issue. From its very nature, evolution is beyond proof." Prof. Whitney of Yale University says, "Those are perhaps the worst foes to its success who are overhasty to take it and use it as a proved fact." **Practically all leading evolutionists**, with the possible exception of Prof. Ernst Haeckel, of Jena, admit that evolution is unproven.

QUESTIONS WHICH MUST BE ANSWERED

LeConte's definition mentions "changes," "certain laws," and "resident forces." A change must have a force to produce it, Whence came the force? When did a law ever make itself? Where there is a law, there must be a lawmaker. When did a force ever create itself? Reason tells us that it must have had a Cause or a Creator.

Evolution is not merely a growth, as of a fruit from a bud; it is not a simple progression as the metamorphosis of the butterfly from the worm. The bud IS the immature fruit, as the worm is the undeveloped butterfly. Evolution involves the formation of new and entirely distinct species of plants and animals, brought into being by certain inscrutable forces, which came we know not how nor whence, operating ceaselessly and uniformly in the past as in the present. And yet, strange to say, we see NO evidence of it anywhere in nature.

There must have been an incalculable number of intermediate forms between the different species, but **none** of these have ever been found, although the search for them has been carried on in the air, on the earth, and under the earth.

THE CREDULOUS EVOLUTIONIST

Geology, that much abused and misinterpreted science, throws no light on the question, but although we are devoid of proof, those who refuse to accept the dictum of non-christian scientists and their theological disciples, are classed as ignorant, credulous, and old-fashioned. Who is the more credulous, the man who accepts a theory with no known facts to support it—absolutely none—or he who refuses allegiance to an hypothesis until he is shown some reliable evidence of its truth?

CAMOUFLAGE

We are reminded of the progress in knowledge, of the progress in civilization, of the changes in the social system, and in man's views of God, and are asked to take these as proofs of the evolution of the human body from that of the brute, although it is difficult to see any connection between them. It would be easy to prove that Degeneration, not Evolution, is a fact in art, literature, physical development, and intellectual

EVOLUTION AND THE BIBLE

equipment generally, notwithstanding that we have the morning paper laid at our door, and possess the aeroplane, the wireless telegraph, and the radio-telephone.

THE EVOLUTIONIST ASKS A LITTLE HELP FROM GOD

Some evolutionists like A. R. Wallace allow God to step in at various points, and change the non-living to the living, the plant to the animal, and the animal to the man. But they still adhere to the belief that new species are formed by these "progressive changes" and "resident forces." They are silent when asked why we do not see any such transformations today, if and when, as they assure us, the same forces are working.

Haeckel is consistent in that he says that if the Creator is admitted at any point, He may as well be admitted all along, but not many of his followers are as honest. Those who have not given much study to this subject may not have the right to reject the evolutionist's conclusions, but they surely may be allowed the privilege of requesting some evidence or proof of his assertions, and for a sight of at least a few intermediate forms.

SCHOLARSHIP

We are assured that "the consensus of scholarship" has accepted evolution. Let him beware who dares to contradict this statement! When we quote the names of many great scientists who have utterly repudiated this idea, as unproven, unprovable, and entirely wrong, we are told with an air of scorn for our ignorance, that these authorities are not in the same class with those on the other side.

Some theistic evolutionists quote Henry Drummond's "Ascent of Man," and seem to believe that Drummond's opinion is of considerable authority in the scientific world.

Drummond wrote this book in 1893—29 years ago—so that from a scientific standpoint, it is quite out of date. He, of course, was not an original investigator, but simply an enthusiastic follower of Darwin, impressed by a theory which was at that time novel and interesting, but which has been completely discredited, even by evolutionists, as will be pointed out later in this article.

George Adam Smith, in his "Life of Henry Drummond," says on page 435, "This book (The Ascent of Man) is the work of a **poetic translator** of the science of his time, rather than of an original scientific thinker."

Professor McKendrick, of the Chair of Physiology in the University of Glasgow, a sympathetic contemporary of Drummond, wrote; "One cannot help feeling that Prof. Drummond reads into the phenomena of nature some of his own mental moods."

Drummond's book was a complete recantation of the principal philosophic heresy of another, earlier and better known work of his, "Natural Law in the Spiritual World." The main argument of this latter book rested upon two unproved and impossible assumptions, and Drummond himself became much discontented with it.

This fact is mentioned to show that the author, while no doubt a sincere Christian, was impetuous and impressionable in forming his opinions, and, in this case at least, was carried away by the strange but fascinating Darwinian conception of man's origin. His views were constantly changing, and "The Ascent of Man" was chiefly an elaboration of certain of Darwin's theories, expressed in attractive and arresting language, which gave the book a popular appeal. The hypotheses he espoused have long since been discarded by scientific leaders.

We may be sure that if Drummond were living today, and had at his disposal the accumulated evidence of thirty years of experiment and discovery, he would consider his "Ascent of Man" with its fantastic speculations, nothing more than a childish fairy-tale.

A FALSEHOOD NAILED

The opinions of world-renowned men like Virchow of Berlin, Dawson of Montreal, Etheridge of the British Museum, Groette of Strassburg University, Paulson of Berlin, Clerk Maxwell, Dana, Naegeli, Holliker, Wagner, Snell, Tovel, Bunge the physiological chemist, Brown, Hoffman, and Askernazy, botanists, Oswald Heer, the geologist, Carl Ernst von Baer, the eminent zoologist and anthropologist, Du Bois Reymond, Stuckenburg, and Zockler and a host of others, have no weight. It seems to be a fact that NO opinion from whatever source, no matter how weighty or learned, is of any account with those who are consumed with the determination to reject the Bible at any cost, and shut God out of His universe. Scholarship is not on the side of the evolutionist, notwithstanding the loud and repeated proclamation of this falsehood.

THE ORIGIN OF SPECIES

There are some things which must have occurred if evolution is true. New species must have been formed from pre-existing species. This is the basis of the whole theory, and was Darwin's field of labor. It may be said to be fundamental.

And yet there are two admitted fatal defects. First, not one single instance of the evolution of a species is known, and second, no law or force by which such changes could take place, has been discovered. **Darwin himself**, in his "Life and Letters," Vol. III. P. 25, says, "There are two or three millions of species

EVOLUTION AND THE BIBLE

on earth, sufficient field one might think for observation. But it must be said today, that in spite of all the efforts of trained observers, not one change of species into another is on record."

Huxley, Tyndall, Prof. Winchell, Prof Conn, and many other evolutionist authorities might be quoted to the same effect. Why is this? Surely, SURELY, we have a right to expect these, and they MUST exist if evolution be true. If the fish is changing into the reptile, and the reptile into the bird, the bird into the mammal, and the mammal into the man, we ought to have little difficulty in finding, at least, ONE instance. But we ask in vain for a glimpse of even a single specimen. This fact alone should be sufficient to discredit the whole fantastic theory, but the credulous believer in the brute-ancestry idea, closes his eyes to facts. He strains at the gnat, but easily swallows the camel.

CONFLICTING THEORIES—THEIR OBJECT

The cause of the "resident force" which is said to result in evolution, is entirely undiscovered. Various schools offer different and weird explanations, all combatted and rejected by others. Theory after theory is invented in a frantic effort to find some explanation of the existence of plant and animal life, other than that of the Bible. The object seems to be to discredit Genesis. Then, we may do what we like with the remaining books of the Bible, because their source is human. Exclude God from the process of Creation as far as possible, destroy faith in His infallible supervision of the words and thoughts of the Book bearing His name, and the result is freedom of thought and conduct on the part of man.

MAN

It makes him not a dependent creature, but an inherently divine being, who by his own innate power, has mastered almost insuperable obstacles, has raised himself from the lowest stage to the highest, and is on the way to still greater achievements.. The Bible tells us, on the other hand, that "man was born in sin and shapen in iniquity," that he is a lost sinner with no power to save himself, and that his ultimate restoration can come from no good works of his own, but simply and solely by the grace of God, manifested in the propitiatory sacrifice of Jesus Christ. This is always displeasing to human pride. Therefore, anything is welcome which makes it possible to disregard these objectionable, old-fashioned passages as not divinely inspired.

SCIENCE QUARRELS WITH ITSELF

The pathway of science is strewn with discarded theories once accepted as facts. True science is certain about very few things indeed, and the Bible contradicts none of them.

We hear much of a warfare between science and theology, but it would be more apropos to speak of the wars between the theories of science. In his 83rd year, Herbert Spencer said, "I wish in my heart I had never heard of the intellectual man with his science, philosophy and logic."

THE FAILURES OF EVOLUTION

Evolution fails to account for many things which must be explained. Some of these are the origin of matter, the origin of force, the formation and orderly arrangement of the universe, and the origin of life.

Spencer says that the originator of matter is the "UNKNOWABLE," thus confessing that his great philosophy rests on what he does not and cannot know. Darwin said on this point, "I am in a hopeless muddle." Until something better than the Bible solution of the difficulty is offered, we shall refuse to fix our faith on anything which is mythical and unknowable.

When evolution is asked to account for the great forces which animate the universe, such as gravity, heat, motion, and light, it is dumb. If we are informed that they are laws of Nature, we are still in the dark because every law must have a law-maker. What is this dynamic Something which energises the universe? The evolutionist says "Nature", which means nothing. The sensible man says, "God," and his intellect is satisfied.

Evolution fails to account for the marvellous and orderly movement of the heavenly bodies which whirl in their orbits with the accuracy of a chronometer. There is no collision, no noise. "There is no speech nor language, their voice is not heard."

THE NEBULAR HYPOTHESIS—A FANTASY

The nebular theory, now the only one in favor with scientists in opposition to the Mosaic record, assumes that the universe began in a mass of fire-mist, a ball of gas which contracted,—contrary to all known laws of gases—and from some unknown cause, force and motion developed sufficient heat, until it became a whirling, molten ball, and threw off the myriads of worlds we call stars, all moving in their tremendous orbits, smoothly and accurately, and yet without any hand to guide or direct. All these assumptions involve us in insoluble mysteries and self-contradictions which hopelessly baffle the intellect and explain nothing.

Whence came the fire-mist? Whence that mysterious power which prevents collision and chaos? The materialist says, "I do not know." The Christian says, "God." Which is more reasonable?

EVOLUTION AND THE BIBLE

LIFE, WHENCE?—GOD NECESSARY

The origin of life is an unexplainable problem to the evolutionist. To say that self-operating "resident forces" united the four gases, carbon, hydrogen, nitrogen, and oxygen, and a few other less commonly known elements, without the direct act of a Creator, and that this combination resulted in life, requires an amazing credulity which, we admit, we do not possess. If a Creator be allowed at the beginning, then, as Haeckel says, He may as well be admitted all along the process.

EVOLUTION'S MONUMENTAL FAILURE

Here then, is the greatest failure of all on the part of evolution. And yet, this is its favorite field, on which depends the whole theory. If there was a God who originated life, the single cell, the simplest living creature from which the believer in evolution starts his upward climb, how much greater faith does it require to believe that He created perfect plants and animals in the first place, as we have them today? One is as mysterious as the other, but just as simple to One who possessed the power of producing life. Certainly all the EVIDENCE goes to prove that there has been no change of species since the first Creation.

THE HERRING ACROSS THE TRAIL

Variations innumerable, there are of course, but a variation is not a species, much as the evolutionist would like to have it so.

IMPASSABLE BIOLOGICAL BARRIERS

There are certain biological barriers which confront the evolutionist, and which he must remove before we can accept his theory. These are the difference between plants and animals; the difference between vertebrates (animals with a backbone), and invertebrates (animals without a backbone); and the difference between mammals and all other vertebrates.

ANOTHER QUESTIONAIRE

1. How was the animal kingdom produced? Here is involved the introduction into matter, of sensation and consciousness. Plants live, animals live and feel, and have consciousness. At this point, every sensible person must admit the intervention of an outside Power which has altered matter and endowed it with new qualities. Wallace says, "Here we are impressed with the certainty that something new has arisen,—a being whose nascent consciousness has gone on increasing in power and definiteness until it has culminated in the higher animals. No explanation, or attempt at explanation, such as the statement

that life is the result of the molecular forces of the protoplasm; or that the whole existing organic universe, from the amoeba up to the man was latent in the fire-mist from which the solar system was developed—can afford any mental satisfaction, or help in any way to a solution of the mystery."

2. How came the backbone? All animals are divided into two groups, those without a backbone, and those with one. How could a butterfly become a bird, a snail a serpent, or a jelly-fish acquire the skeleton of a shark? Science has absolutely no answer.

3. Whence came the breast? Vertebrates are either mammals (animals with breasts with which to suckle their young), or submammals. The breastless tribes are birds, reptiles, and fishes. They are comparatively low down in the animal scale, when compared with the mammal, which gives nourishment to its offspring, and stands erect and apart from the inferior class.

Is it possible to explain how an animal who never got milk from its mother, stumbled by chance on a new method of giving what itself had never received or been taught? The breast stands as an impossible barrier to the evolutionist, and there is no animal which in any way can be regarded as a connecting link between these two master-groups. If the process is in force today, as we are told, we should see, somewhere, some animals with rudimentary breasts in process of development. But we look in vain.

ONE WAY OUT?

The theistic evolutionist allows God to intervene at these crucial points, and make the necessary changes. But if a special creative act of God is needed here, why not accept the record of Genesis which says that the various species of plants and animals were created, each "after its own kind," especially since there is no evidence to the contrary? If special creative acts are necessary, what becomes of the hypothesis of evolution? It is absolutely unnecessary.

MAN AND BEAST—AN UNBRIDGED GULF

Then, the problem of MAN must be considered. He is separated from all other members of his class (mammalian) by an impassable gulf. He alone has a perfect brain, capable of producing language, and with the capacity for progress and culture. He alone possesses a mind with faculties of reason, imagination and art. Above all, he alone has been endowed with a moral and spiritual nature which raises him far above the brute.

These faculties could not have been developed by the oft-mentioned evolutionary forces. It is inconceivable that the intellect

EVOLUTION AND THE BIBLE

of a Shakespeare, or the moral nature of a Paul, could have been potentially existent in the star-fish or the jelly fish, only waiting for proper conditions and environment to evolve into the marvellous organ which man possesses. It is a preposterous assumption, and yet we find the doctrine enunciated in the school text-books, the Sunday newspaper supplements, and taught to the youth of our country as an established fact. Surely, this is the climax of ignorant credulity.

MODERN BIOLOGICAL CONCLUSIONS

Whither, then, do the latest and best Biological conclusions lead us? For many years, the evolutionary Biologist has been chasing up one blind alley after another, in an endeavor to find some explanation of the origin of the various species of plants and animals, other than that of sudden and perfect Creation recorded in Genesis. He has been making frantic attempts to capture a tantalizing and elusive will-o-the-wisp.

DISCARDED THEORIES AND A LOST TRAIL

Weissman discredited the Lamarckian theory of the inheritance of acquired characters, and Mendel's Law disposed of the theory of the accumulation of successive fluctuating variations, so that modern Biology seems to be lost among the fogs of its ever-changing and incredible hypotheses. At present it is trying to find the main trail which was lost when the new discarded teachings of Lyell and Darwin led it blindly and hopelessly off the right track.

RESEMBLANCE IN STRUCTURE—NO PROOF OF HEREDITY

The evolutionist followers of Haeckel, et al, arguing from what they call the recapitulation theory, arrange life in three groups, the embryonic, geologic, and taxonomic or classification series. They ask us to notice the resemblances between the varying forms of life, and then they explain these singular resemblances by assuring us that all the higher forms have simply developed from the lower. They tell us that the embryonic, or immature, unborn, developing animal, passes through the various successive stages, through which its ancestors passed during the long ages of its biologic history. We are informed that by an innumerable succession of minute changes, or perhaps by sudden "jumps," the different species have undoubtedly been formed. The simplest form of life has gradually changed into the most complex, the crown and apex of all, being MAN.

These changes are brought about by NATURAL SELECTION, SURVIVAL of the FITTEST (perhaps), and of course the transmission of acquired characteristics.

A very recent issue of the Scientific American says, that embryologists have had to give up the theory of recapitulation, because of the many striking instances now known it cannot apply. "The critical comments of such embryologists as Hertwig, Keibel, and Vialleton, have practically torn to shreds the aforesaid fundamental biogenetic law. Its almost unanimous abandonment has left considerably at a loss those investigators who sought in the structure of organisms, the key to their remote origin or to their relationships." (February, 1921; p. 121.)

THE DEATH-BED OF DARWINISM—DEATH CERTIFICATE GRANTED BY EVOLUTIONISTS

Here we stand at the death-bed of what has repeatedly been called the strongest argument in favor of Biologic evolution.

John Burroughs, the veteran naturalist, wrote in "The Atlantic Monthly" a short time ago, "Darwin has already been shorn of his selection doctrines as completely as Samson was shorn of his locks." (August, 1920; p. 237).

Robert Heath Lock, a recognized English authority, in his book, "Recent Progress in the Study of Variation, Heredity, and Evolution," a revised edition of which was issued not long since under the editorial name of Professor Doncaster, says, on page 61, "It does not necessarily follow that natural selection, directing the accumulation of minute differences, has been the method by which these adapted forms have been originated."

Professor William Bateson, perhaps the greatest living Biologist, in a revolutionary address before the American Association for the Advancement of Science, in Toronto on the evening of December 28th, 1921, utterly repudiated Darwinism with its theory of natural selection and survival of the fittest, and denied that any new species had ever been formed from pre-existing species. Bateson is Director of the John Innes Horticultural Institute, Surrey, England, and there is no one living whose opinion carries more or perhaps equal weight. Other authorities might be quoted indefinitely to the same effect.

Haeckel, speaking of Darwin's indispensable doctrine of acquired characters, says, "Belief in the inheritance of acquired characters is a necessary axiom of the monistic creed;" and he further declared that rather than agree with August Weissman, E. Ray Lankester, and Alfred Russell Wallace in denying the inheritance of acquired characters, "it would be better to accept a mysterious Creation of all the species as described in the Mosaic account."

Herbert Spencer also left himself on record as follows: "Close contemplation of the facts impresses me more strongly than ever

EVOLUTION AND THE BIBLE

with the two alternatives, either there has been inheritance of acquired characters, or there has been no Evolution."

Persevering and exhaustive experiments on uncounted thousands of guinea pigs, rats, mice, rabbits, pigeons, and great numbers of other animals, have been made in an effort to prove that acquired characters are actually transmitted in heredity, to at least a slight degree. J. Arthur Thompson, an acknowledged evolutionistic authority, in the latest edition of his book "Heredity," summarises the present scientific situation of this aspect of the case as follows, "Have we any concrete evidence to warrant us believing that definite modifications are ever, as such or in any representative degree, transmitted? It appears to us that WE HAVE NOT."

Thus we see that Biology which has been searching vainly for some reasonable and scientific explanation which will discredit the Bible account of Creation, is at last compelled to retrace its steps from the devious byways into which it has strayed, and get back to the main road. This main road seems to lead straight towards the long discarded doctrine of a real Creation.

GEOLOGY

What is the testimony of Geology? Does it support the evolutionary theory, or does a correct interpretation of the facts it has uncovered disprove and discredit the theory? Let us see.

The principal argument for the development of the higher types of life from lower organisms is based upon a study of the fossil remains which the geologists have discovered in the rocky layers. The confident assertion is made that the older the strata in the earth's surface, the simpler are the forms imbedded therein; the more recent the strata, the more complex and highly developed are the remains of plant and animal life. This is quoted as an axiom in almost all the scientific school text books.

Here we are confronted with a straight issue. Either the rocks bear this testimony to the truth of the evolutionary theory or they do not. Prof. Downey of Chicago goes so far as to say that this is the one primary argument, the others being simply corroborative.

THE HOUSE OF CARDS

Geologists have reared an imposing structure in their efforts to bolster up the wobbling theory of evolution, but when we examine it closely, we find that it is nothing but a house of cards, which is toppled over by the first breeze of common-sense investigation and interpretation.

There are preserved in the rocks thousands of specimens of

both animals and plants. There are lowly organisms of the crab and cuttle-fish variety, and more highly organized forms, fishes, lizards, sloths, and bones of great monsters now extinct. The evolutionist says that the simplest forms are always found in the lowest strata, and the most complex in the recent or superficial strata. So, they tell us, they have developed.

Hugh Miller, one of the earliest and most famous palaentologists, in his brilliant book, "Old Red Sandstone," recently republished, says, "It is a law of nature that the chain of being from the lowest to the highest form of life, should be in some degree, a continuous chain; that the various classes of existence should shade into one another, so that it often proves a matter of no little difficulty to point out the exact line of demarcation where one class of family ends, and another class or family begins. The naturalist passes from the vegetable to the animal tribes, scarcely aware, amid the perplexing forms of intermediate existence, at what point he quits the precincts of the one, to enter on those of the other. All the animal families have in like manner their connecting links; and it is chiefly out of these that writers like Lamarck and Maillet construct their system. **They confound gradation with progress.** Geoffrey Hudson was a very short man, and Goliath of Gath a very tall one; and the gradations of human stature lie between. But gradation is not progress; and though we find full grown men of five feet, five feet six inches, and six feet and a half, the fact gives us no earnest whatever that the race is rising in stature, and that at some future period the average height of the human family will be somewhere between ten and eleven feet. And equally unsound is the argument that from a principle of gradation in races, we may reduce a principle of progress in races. The tall man of six feet need entertain as little hope of rising into eleven feet as the short man of five; nor has the fish that occasionally flies any better chance of passing into a bird than the fish that only swims. Geology abounds in creatures of the intermediate class. But it **FURNISHES NO GENEALOGICAL LINK TO SHOW THAT THE EXISTENCES OF ONE RACE DERIVE THEIR LINEAGE FROM THE EXISTENCES OF ANOTHER.** The scene shifts as we pass from one formation to another; we are introduced in each to new dramatis personae. Of all vertebrates,, fish rank lowest, and in geological history appear first. Now, fishes differ very much among themselves; some rank nearly as low as worms; some as nearly as high as reptiles; and if fish could have risen into reptiles, and reptiles into mammalia, we would necessarily expect to find lower forms of fish passing into higher, and taking precedence of the higher in their appearance in point of time. If such be not the case, if fish made their first appearance, not in their least perfect, but in their most perfect state, not in their nearest approximation to the worm, but in their nearest approximation to the reptile, there is no room for progression, and the argument falls. Now, it is a geological fact that fish of the higher orders appear first on the stage, and that they are found to occupy exactly the same level during the vast period represented by five succeeding formations (many millions of years as estimated by the geologist)."

"There is no progression. If fish rose into reptiles, it must have been by rapid transformation. There is no getting out of the miracle in the case; there is no alternative between creation and metamorphosis. The infidel substitutes progression for deity. ..Geology robs him of his God."

NO INTERMEDIATE FORMS

It is a fact beyond controversy that there is a complete absence in the geological record of those transitional forms, the gradual modifications linking the various species of animals and plants in a finely graduated system, with thousands of forms showing in rudimentary structure those organs, which in the more advanced forms have become fully developed.

These forms SHOULD exist and should easily be found if evolution is a fact. But in spite of the most persistent and painstaking search by the most expert and trained investigators, there is no trace of these intermediate stages.

DARWIN'S CONFESSION

Darwin admitted this fact. He said, "Geology assuredly does not reveal any such finely graduated organic chain; and this perhaps is the most obvious and gravest objection which can be urged against my theory." And here, let us agree, "Mr. Darwin said something."

A FOSSIL SCIENCE

George McCready Price, Prof. of Geology, Pacific Union College, California, has shown most conclusively, and his logical arguments based upon indisputable facts have not been refuted—that the "current cosmological geology is a fossil science, an out-of-date method, a survival of a by-gone age."

As he states in the introduction to "Fundamentals of Geology," "In any healthy science, the fundamental theories are always kept well adjusted to all the new discoveries, for when this is not done, a science is soon in comatose condition. For nearly a century geology has never revised its fundamental theories."

There is urgent need of the complete reformation of the science of geology, in view of recent discoveries mentioned by many great scientists like George Frederick Wright and Eduard Suess, perhaps the greatest living geologist, who, in his masterly work, "The Face of the Earth," enumerates instance after instance of rock formation and fossil deposits completely upsetting the old geological interpretations, which for many years have been used by evolutionists as their chief arguments.

DARWINISM FALLS—WITHOUT THE SUCCESSION-OF-LIFE IDEA

Darwinism, as a part, a minor part, of the general evolutionary theory, rests logically and historically on the succession-of-life idea as taught by geology. That is, geology has taught us that there has been a regular succession of life on the globe in a very definite order, the simpler forms appearing in the older and deeper strata, and the more highly developed in the recent strata.

If this succession of life is not an actual scientific fact capable of the clearest proof, then Darwinism or any other form of bilogical evolution can have no more scientific value than the vagaries of the old Greeks. As an inductive science, it would necessarily be a gigantic blunder, hardly second to the Ptolemaic astronomy.

THEN AND NOW—PAST AND PRESENT

Price has shattered the old idea of Uniformity, viz., that the natural processes and changes of the past ages are the same as those operating today. He, along with Suess and Howorth, has demonstrated conclusively and for all time that there is nothing now going on in our modern world at all explanatory of even the last and least of these great geological changes of the past. He emphasizes among others, three remarkable facts, about the order in which the fossils occur, which plainly contradict the current theories.

SKIPPING

These are: (1) "Very many genera, often whole tribes, of animals and plants, are found as fossils only in the so-called "oldest" rocks, and have skipped all the other formations, though found in comparative abundance in our modern world. Many other kinds have skipped from the Mesozoic down, while innumerable others skip large sections of the geological series.

"These obvious absurdities would be easily avoided by saying that the current distinctions between the fossils as to age are purely artificial and conventional, just as is the modern taxonomic or classification series. In the light of this fact, at least, one kind of fossil is intrinsically just as old or just as young as another."

EVOLUTION AND THE BIBLE

UNEXPLAINABLE GAPS

2. "It is a very common thing to find "young" beds, say some of the Tertiaries, in such perfect conformability on some of the "oldest" beds, say some of the Cambrian or Devonian, that the vast interval of time alleged to be properly intervening between them is utterly unrepresented either by deposition or by erosion. It is as if nature had closed shop or put an injunction on the action of the elements for a hundred million years or so, and everything had to continue in the status quo ante for all this long interval, the waters neither wearing away nor building up over any part of this taboo ground for all this time. In many instances, too, these age-separated formations are so much alike in structure and in mineral make-up that, "were it not for fossil evidence, one would naturally think that a single formation was being dealt with" (McConnell), while these tell-tale conditions are "not merely local, but persistent over wide areas" (Geikie), so much so that the "numerous examples" (Suess) of these anomalous conditions "may well be cause for astonishment" (Seuss).

When conformability is spoken of, what is meant is that the layers or strata are lying one upon the other with absolutely no evidence of any change since they were first deposited. All the strata which geologists tell us are found between "young" or recent, and "old" layers, are missing in innumerable instances. Millions of years elapsed, so we are told, between these two formations. Did Nature take a holiday for that long period in certain sections? Geological uniformity is a myth and a delusion.

"Often, too, these conformable relations of incongruous strata are repeated over and over again in the same vertical section, the same kind of anachronistic strata reappearing alternately with others of an entirely different 'age,' that is, repeatedly appearing, 'as if regularly interbedded' (A. Geikie) with them, in a series of strata that obviously have never been disturbed.

"UPSIDE DOWN" CONDITIONS

3. "In numerous instances, and spreading over hundreds or even thousands of square miles of area, 'older' strata are found on top of 'younger' strata, and with just as much appearance of conformability. That is, all the physical appearances indicate that these beds were actually laid down in this order, an order so flatly contradicting the alleged 'ages' of the popular theory.

"One of the largest areas of this character extends from about the middle of Montana northward along the line of the Rockies to the Yellowhead Pass in Alberta, and is wide enough in some places to comprise several parallel ranges of mountains. The mass of these mountains is composed of Algonkian limestone, while the underlying beds, or the beds comprising the intervening valleys, are Cretaceous. The total area involved is some ten thousand square miles, and the mountains look like Palaeozoic (Algonkian) islands floating on a Cretaceous sea.

"But these Algonkian rocks are supposed to be the very oldest fossiliferous rocks on earth, while the Cretaceous rocks are among those classified as quite 'young.' But these Algonkian rocks are on top, while the theory says that they ought to be at the bottom. And the Cretaceous are at the bottom, while the theory says they ought to be on top. Thus, either the rocks are wrong, or the theory is wrong.

"Strange to say, evolutionary scientists prefer to believe that the rocks are wrong, and that nature is here trying to deceive us, as it were, rather than to admit the possibility of their theory being at fault.

"But these conditions are not at all the only ones. Several other localities have been found in Wyoming, Utah, and Idaho where these 'upside down' conditions prevail. Other similar examples occur in the Appalachian Mountains, in the Grampians, in the Alps, and in fact in almost every region that has been at all well explored.

THE SILENCES OF SCIENCE

"Ordinary scientific literature is strangely silent in regard to these things. Evolutionists always speak of them 'sub rosa,' and with extreme reluctance. But how could anything be imagined more absolutely conclusive against the whole vain scheme which has for these many years set itself squarely in opposition to the Word of God? For if these rocks, covering almost a State, and that have every physical appearance of being in a normal order, were really deposited in the order in which we find them. the whole system of biological evolution is a mass of moonshine, merely another elaborate blunder, soon to take its rightful place alongside the many other sad wrecks of human speculations which dot the shores of scientific and philosophic history, wrecks which were once the fond pride of their inventors, but which now have become merely object lessons, 'to paint a moral or adorn a tale.'

SCIENTIFIC (?) CREDULITY

"In the light of these facts, is it not amazing to see the confiding, child-like faith with which other educated people receive the ipse dixit of any geologist regarding the exact 'age' of any particular rock deposit? Why is it still possible for the fantastic speculation regarding the exact order in which the various types of animals appeared on earth. to be received by

EVOLUTION AND THE BIBLE

intelligent people with all the solemn confidence which attaches to a chemical analysis or the prediction of an eclipse?

CREATION—A FACT

"All the facts lead us inevitably to the conclusion that there has been a literal Creation, since modern science has forever outgrown the idea of spontaneous generation, and in the light of all recent facts, there is absolutely nothing upon which to build a scheme of evolution. Inductive geology is utterly unable to show that certain types of life originated before others. With the myth of a life succession, dissipated once and forever, the world today stands face to face with **Creation as a direct act of the Infinite God.**

THE BLIND LEADING THE BLIND—THE DITCH?

And yet the evolutionist says, as quoted from Graebner's "Evolution": "The science of Paleontology (the study of fossil remains) furnishes the basic argument for our hypothesis, the older the strata of the earth's surface, the simpler the fossils found therein. This sounds impressive. But we ask him: 'How do you know the age of the strata?' And the answer is: 'That, of course, is the business of the geologist to determine.' We now turn to the geologist and ask: 'How do you determine the age of the strata?' And the geologist answers: 'Why, evolutionary science has proved that the simplest animals and plants appeared first, hence, where I find simple fossils, I know that I have a more ancient bed of limestone or sandstone than the strata which contains more complex forms, which appeared later.' Note well, the geologists assert that this is the best and final proof for the position of a stratum in the scale of geological history. The geologist depends on the fossils. But he believes these to belong to an earlier or more recent age because he accepts the evolutionist's word for it. And the evolutionist says: 'The geologist tells me these rocks are oldest, but in them I find the simplest forms; hence the evolutionary theory is proven.'

The geologist leans on the evolutionist, and the evolutionist on the geologist, the one accepting the unproven hypotheses of the other as the basis of his argument. Two broken reeds! How can a thinking person be deceived by any such method of reasoning as this?

Is not this a **very, very** extraordinary situation? How can the evolutionist quote the geologist when the geologist asserts that he classifies his layers of rock according to the fossils, and that he accepts what the evolutionist says regarding these?

Surely this disposes of both the evolutionist's argument from the fossils, and also the "ages" of speculative geology.

There are one or two further considerations which are important. One concerns rudimentary organs.

RUDIMENTARY ORGANS

Darwinism does not account for the fact that the various organs of animals, while in process of evolution, must have been, through many generations, in a rudimentary, incomplete state. Since it is a basic doctrine of evolution that useful variations were transmitted from parent to offspring **because they were useful;** and furthermore, since only the **fully** developed eye, the **hearing** ear, etc., were useful, it is not possible to understand how these organs in their rudimentary state, when useless to the animal for seeing, hearing, etc., could serve any purpose which would make their transmission advantageous to the species.

As a matter of fact, there is no known law whereby they could have been evolved. If these organs, as many of them are, were necessary to the life of the animal, then, while the organs were rudimentary and useless, the animals must have perished, and the species would have been speedily exterminated—before it was born!

This difficulty of rudimentary structure presents **an insuperable obstacle to the acceptance of the evolutionary hypothesis, even on scientific grounds.**

INSTINCT

The same kind of obstacle is presented in the various instincts of animals, the homing instinct of birds and insects, the building instinct, the migrating instinct, etc. How could they possibly have been developed through forces working by natural selection or any other law?

On instinct depends the existence of most animals. According to the theory, these instincts have been developed by slow degrees, hence there must have been a very long time when these instincts, because not yet completely developed, were useless to the animal. But if useless, the animal must have perished, and so evolution is ruled out as the process by which they were developed. **They must have been implanted in the animal at the first moment of life. That means a sudden Creation, just as recorded in Genesis.**

THE MISSING LINK—ALWAYS MISSING!

All of the many missing links which have at different times been heralded as the intermediate forms between man and beast, have turned out to be definitely animal or definitely human remains, but still the unwearying search goes on. Expeditions—called scientific—are being dispatched to all likely corners of the earth. "Hope springs eternal in the human breast,"

EVOLUTION AND THE BIBLE

but, "He that sitteth in the heavens" laughs at man's audacious and impudent attempt to disprove the veracity of His book. Because the skeleton of animals is constructed on a similar plan to that of man, is no proof that he is descended from the animal. Similarity in structure does not prove heredity. Surely, the Creator may be allowed to adopt the same general scheme of structure in forming different species. This favourite argument, which appeals to many people, is really very trivial and unconvincing.

GENESIS—MYTH OR TRUTH?

In closing, let me say a few words in regard to the early chapters of Genesis which are called mythical or poetical parables, not actual historical fact. The battle today is perhaps not so much as to theories of inspiration, but rather as to the accuracy and trustworthiness of the Bible itself. Taking **Genesis** for the moment, it is recognized by all authorities to be most remarkable for its absolutely complete accord with the best modern science. Its language, understood by all ages, is so worded that it **contradicts no positively known scientific fact, and in addition, proclaims truths thousands of years in advance of the time in which it was written.** Even Prof. Ernst Haeckel had to admit that the simple, grand and logical ideas of the Hebrew Lawgiver have never been surpassed.

THE WONDERFUL SCIENCE OF GENESIS

Herbert Spencer wrote of the **five ultimate categories**, that is, the five most complete forms in which our knowledge of the Unknowable, as he rather paradoxically phrased it, may be expressed. We find them **all in Genesis.**

1. Space. "God created the heavens."
2. Time. "In the beginning."
3. Matter. '"The earth."
4. Motion. "The Spirit of God moved on the face of the waters."
5. Force. Suggested both in the phrase about the Spirit of God, and in the very name of God, derived from a Hebrew root signifying strength, and meaning "the putter forth of power."

Here we have the most considered and systematized philosophy of the twentieth century, the crown and apex of all the thinking that men have been doing since they have been on the earth. After years of laborious study, inheriting all that had come down through the ages, Spencer wrote these things down in much detail. We turn to Genesis and find them all there in three short sentences. There is the flower of all his philosophy lying at the foundation of all the thoughts that the simplest believer in the Word of God has ever entertained of these great and lofty themes.

Dr. A. R. Wallace proved that only this earth of ours, out of all possible or actual worlds, is suitable for the production and upholding of life as we know it. The Christian has sense as well as science on his side when he claims that these things reveal a directing and designing Mind, and that this Mind is God.

HOW DID MOSES DO IT?

The stated order of Creation—15 definite things, as mentioned by Moses—is absolutely in accord with the most recent science. According to the Law of Permutation, when Moses reached the fifteenth creative act, there were more than thirteen thousand million possible orders, and yet in all of them he makes not a single mistake.

How can this be explained if we suppose that Moses wrote simply as a man, knowing only the science of that day? Reason tells us that only God, the Creator, could have revealed this information to him.

Nothing has ever been discovered which in any way impairs the credibility of the Genesis narrative, and we marvel at the fact that we find a man writing more than three milleniums ago, who has been preserved from the errors and ignorance which lie scattered thickly over the history of human thought. Moses is one of the outstanding figures of all time, and we bow our heads and hearts before this record as the very Word of God.

WHERE EVOLUTION LEADS

The acceptance of the theory of evolution involves, naturally, the rejection of the idea of Creation as described in the Bible, and with it—although this is disputed—at least a partial denial of a personal God, intimately concerned in the life and welfare of His creatures. Immanuel Kant threw this notion on the junk pile, a century or so ago, and practically all the universities of the world have, for a hundred years, taught their pupils to regard Kant as second to no other human being as a teacher of wisdom. The theistic evolutionist must necessarily attribute to God an act which only a fiendish Omnipotent Being would commit. This God must have implanted in the primordial life-germ the tendency to sin, causing all the misery and woe under which the world now groans. The responsibility for all sin rests upon Him, and man is simply the unfortunate and undeserving victim of a dastardly deed, committed by One who had the power to incorporate into our ancestral protoplasm the sinning capacity, or to refrain from so doing. The evolutionist has decided that this Omniscient First Cause chose to curse us with the power of variation towards evil.

NO FALL—NO REDEEMER

Hence, we must throw overboard the concept of the Fall of

EVOLUTION AND THE BIBLE

man—according to evolution there has been no Fall, but a constant ascent. If there be no Fall, then no Redemption is required. If no Redemption, no Christ as Saviour. In fact, the essential Deity of the Son of God is denied. We have no inspired Bible, simply a collection of human writings, more or less interesting, containing certain ethical truths, and profitable for doctrine and teaching. But, its exhortations come to us without any extraordinary authority, because, only in a few instances, perhaps in none, are they actually from God.

MAN—HIS OWN SAVIOUR

According to this theory, we are masters of our own destinies. We are inherently divine, as Christ was, able to lift ourselves, from the depths, to the heights of some Supreme, Universal, and Impersonal Consciousness, whom we may call God, if we please. A devilish conception, this, which effectively abolishes any necessity for the Atonement of Christ, the central and all-pervading truth of the Bible.

THE RENUNCIATION OF FAITH

In fact, we must renounce ALL the fundamentals of a faith which has proven itself, times without number, to countless thousands throughout all ages, Scriptural, intelligent, reasonable, satisfying, saving us in life, and giving us victory in death.

A STARTLING JUDICIAL CRITICISM BY AN EMINENT MODERN WRITER

A scathing indictment of this scientific falsehood, this "nightmare of waste and death," as Samuel Butler called it, "as baseless as it is repulsive," is found in the American preface to "The Glass of Fashion," a brilliant book, very recently published, from the arresting pen of "A Gentleman with a Duster," author of those almost universally read, and vivid pen pictures, "Mirrors of Downing Street," and "Mirrors of Washington."

This exceptionally observant, literary genius, who is at the same time a wide-awake man of the world, intimately associated with world affairs and most of the modern makers of history, says, in part: "We are held by the philosophical paralysis which has crept over the human mind ever since the dark and disfiguring shadow of Darwinism fell upon the fields of life. Life has lost its way, and there can be no hope of coming into our true inheritance until we have recovered those title-deeds to immortality which our fathers threw away when they set out to wander in the wilderness of this false materialism.

"If we would live we must overthrow this false science which is destroying us, as the fathers of Christianity overthrew paganism, and the fathers of the Renaissance overthrew authority.

"The fashion of daily life is set by those who have sacrificed to a false science, almost without thought, the one great secret of joy, namely, FAITH IN A CREATIVE PURPOSE, FAITH IN MAN'S IMMORTALITY. It is that secret we must recover for mankind, and we can recover it only by making remorseless war on this false science. . . . . Right-thinking, armed with the sword of truth, must destroy wrong-thinking drunk with the dope of Circean lies.

"Our first reason for making war on this false thought is this: It is destroying us; our second reason, that it is not true.

"Darwinism not only justifies the sensualist at the trough and fashion at her glass; it justifies Prussianism at the cannon, and Bolshevism at the prison-door. . . . .

"On these grounds alone Darwinism is condemned; but it is condemned also on scientific grounds. Darwinism explains only the least interesting changes and modifications in physical structure; it does not explain the movement of life nor its manifest direction towards excellence; and as to its origins, and as to the final destination of all this vast and orderly movement of life, it is dumb. Nevertheless this false science, this utterly inadequate theory, which was challenged at the outset, doubted by great men throughout its victorious course of dominion, and which is now acknowledged by every thinker to be but a partial explanation of a few not very important phenomena, still rules the mind of the multitude.

"The mob believes in Darwinian evolution, believes that the universe is an accident, life is an accident, and beauty is an accident. It has made up its mind on hearsay, and incorporated into its moods, without realization of the logical consequences, a theory of existence which is as false as it is destructive. . . . .

"We are in the hands of cynicism. The one insurance against calamity is a new 'climate of opinion,' universal as the air we breathe. The mob must be awakened. The windows of the house of life must be thrown wide open. The mind of humanity must live."

SHALL WE BOW TO BAAL?

In view of all the facts stated herein, are we prepared to make the sacrifice involved in an acceptance of this pagan philosophy, and hypocritically bow the knee, in the name of Christianity, to this modern Baal, this appalling and subtle apostasy, which attempts to deify man and degrade God? I think not. We are driven by the inexorable logic of fact and reason to acknowledge the truth of the sublime statement of the first sentence of Scripture: "In the beginning, God CREATED the heavens and the earth."

EVOLUTION

and the

Blood-Precipitation Test

by

ARTHUR I. BROWN

M.D., C.M., F.R.C.S.E.

PRICE TWENTY-FIVE CENTS

DESIGNED PRODUCTS
149 HARRISON STREET • OAK PARK, ILL.

Printed in U. S. A.

*Affectionately Dedicated to my
very dear friend,*

DR. JOHN L. CAMPBELL

*Dean Bible Department,
Carson-Newman College,
Jefferson City, Tennessee.*

———

*For whose sound advice, unfailing sympathy, and
generous appreciation, the author desires
to express his thanks.*

FOREWORD

This essay, the author believes, is a conclusive answer to those who submit the results of the "Blood-Precipitation Test" as evidence for evolution.

The writer has attempted to put this somewhat technical subject into language which can be understood, after careful reading, by anyone of average intelligence and education. The argument will repay close examination and study.

Prof. L. T. More is Dean of the University of Cincinnati, and Professor of Physics. He is acknowledged to be one of the world's leading physicists. His book, "The Dogma of Evolution," is one of the most powerful ever written on this subject. This book has given the Creationists some of the most effective ammunition they have secured.

Prof. George McCready Price is one of the world's leading Geologists. He has written a number of books including "Fundamentals of Geology," "Q. E. D.," "Back to the Bible," "The Phantom of Organic Evolution," and "The New Geology."

His name will go down in history because of the last-named book, which is, undoubtedly, the sanest, clearest and most irrefutable presentation of the Science of Geology from the standpoint of Creation and the Deluge, ever to see the light of day.

It is a pleasure and privilege to present the endorsations of these two acknowledged scientists, and also the opinion of an eminent religious leader of international reputation, and great scholarship,—the late Dr. John L. Campbell, Dean of the Bible Department of Carson-Newman College, Jefferson City, Tennessee.

Professor Louis Trenchard More writes:

"I thank you very much for the opportunity of reading your paper on 'Blood and Evolution.' I certainly do agree with your main idea that to test the serum prepared from the living animal is not in any way a study of blood as it exists in a living organism. I also agree with you in your final conclusion that unless we are absolutely certain (and we are not certain) that blood from two animals can be chemically similar without having a common ancestor, we have no right to draw inferences which have been drawn. And I feel as you do that it is an unwarranted assumption to suppose that inheritance alone can account for structural resemblances."

Professor George McCready Price says:

"Your article on 'Blood' is absolutely splendid. It is away out of sight of any competitors on this particular subject. It ought to be circulated everywhere, and I hope you will have it printed at once in pamphlet form. It is much needed, and you have done the job so handsomely that no one of the rest of us need tackle this subject, in the way of writing, if you will put this in permanent form."

Dr. J. L. Campbell offers this opinion:

"Your article on the Blood (I am weighing my word) is the ablest thing I have ever read on the whole subject of evolution. I have read and reread it. Your mastery is complete and your refutation more than its weight in gold, and further, I do not know anyone else who could write it."

EVOLUTION AND
THE BLOOD-PRECIPITATION TEST

During the past year or two, and particularly during the past few months, the evidence derived from thousands of highly technical experiments with the blood serum of man and different animals—most of these tests conducted several years ago—(in 1904 to be exact)—has been repeatedly proclaimed as the strongest proof yet discovered in support of the evolution theory.

One reason for this sudden access of enthusiasm for this line of argument may be found in the confusion and doubt among evolutionists because of the decline in value of other alleged "proofs."

Viewed superficially, or by those who do not possess a fair working knowledge of physiology, it seems to offer a rather strong corroboration of transformist claims. On account of its inherent complexity and difficulty it has been somewhat neglected by those who repudiate the idea of a bestial origin for mankind.

Upon a close scientific investigation of the question, with the latest findings of physiology at our disposal, the case for the evolutionist proves to be very weak and his "strong evidence" vanishes before the logic of facts.

As everyone knows, blood is that life-fluid flowing swiftly and ceaselessly through the marvelous system of tiny tubes in our bodies made up of arteries, veins and capillaries. The arteries are the vessels which carry the red oxygenated blood from the heart to all parts of the body. They gradually diminish in size as they branch in a wide network, at last becoming so small that they accommodate but one microscopic cell, in the minute channels known as capillaries which connect the arteries with the veins.

The capillaries are spread out all through the tissues and organs and gather up the flow to discharge into the veins, whose function is to carry the blue blood (blue because loaded with Carbon Dioxide gas instead of Oxygen which has been burnt up in the body) back to the lungs in which it discharges the Carbon Dioxide gas and other impurities to be expelled in breathing. In the lungs it loads up with a fresh supply of Oxygen, again enters the left chamber of the heart and resumes its journey. Back and forth it travels on its round trip constantly varying in its composition as the amount of Oxygen and Carbon Dioxide changes and its food content alters with the continual addition of nourishment and discharge of waste matter.

The food taken into the stomach undergoes the process of digestion by which it is changed into a milky fluid, which is extracted from the intestine by little wide open mouths leading to another series of tubes called lymph channels. These gradually unite into one duct through which the fully digested food, prepared for assimilation and now ready to be absorbed into the system, is emptied into a large vein at the root of the neck, close to the heart.

Blood contains two definite and distinct parts, one solid, the other liquid. The solid portion is composed of small, round, protoplasmic masses called cells, red and white. The red cells derive their color from their contained Haemoglobin, a chemical having a remarkable affinity for Oxygen which it snatches as every opportunity from the oxygen-filled lungs, the air-station through which all the dark carbonated venous blood must pass.

Besides Haemoglobin, the red cells have, like the white, much protoplasm, with its variety of chemicals, to be noticed presently.

The white cells are less numerous than the red,—

one to seven or eight hundred — but are larger, can change their shape and move independently. They have a different and distinct function in devouring invading germs, and perhaps assisting in the manufacture of substances to antagonize the poisons of disease-producing bacteria.

In common with red cells they are composed largely of protoplasm and a group of chemicals.

Protoplasm is the material basis of all living organisms. It is derived, naturally, from the medium which surrounds it, and the elements which compose the body framework must therefore be identical with those found in the earth's crust. The Biblical statement, then, that man was formed from the dust of the earth is verified by physiological investigations.

Every living organism, without exception, contains the following elements which are found also in the ground beneath our feet,—Carbon, Hydrogen, Oxygen, Nitrogen, Sulphur, Phosphorus, Chlorine, Potassium, Sodium, Calcium, Magnesium and Iron.

Some others contain in addition, silicon, iodine, fluorine, bromine, aluminium, manganese and copper.

We see then, that the principal constituents of the blood cells are a large number of chemicals in complex combinations with one another, floating in a fluid medium.

Human blood is made up of rather more than one-third to one-half its weight of corpuscles or cells. It contains from 20 per cent to 25 per cent solids. The liquid part of the blood is named plasma, and this, by clotting, is broken up into serum and a substance called "fibrin"; the latter formed from a normal constituent of the plasma "fibrinogen," which is acted upon by the lime salts of the blood, in the presence of small cells, known as "platelets," thought to be a product of the clotting change. The platelets break up and release "thrombokinase" which combines with another chemical "thrombogen" to form "thrombin." Thrombin unites with fibrinogen, and fibrin — the end result of clotting,—occurs as a fine network of threads which enmesh the cells into a jelly-like mass. This mass falls to the bottom, leaving the serum in the upper portion of the vessel.

Thus, we understand that blood consists of cells and plasma, the plasma made up of serum and fibrinogen. It is necessary constantly to remember that what the scientists are using in their so-called blood tests, is nothing but serum — a small part of blood.

Fibrin forms only one five-hundredth to one two-hundred and fiftieth of the total weight of blood.

The serum contains in 100 parts, 8 to 9 parts of solids, of which seven to eight parts consist of nitrogenous compounds called proteins, while the salts make up about one part.

The chief salt present in the serum is sodium chloride—table salt,—about sixty per cent. Next in order comes sodium carbonate, about 30 per cent, and besides these two we find traces of potassium, sodium, and calcium chlorides, and phosphates. Traces of fats, cholesterin, locithin, dextrose, urea, and other nitrogenous extractives, are constantly found in the serum.

The red corpuscles contain from 30 to 40 per cent total solids, and of the solid constituents, haemoglobin forms nine-tenths. The other tenth corresponds to the framework of protein (Nucleo-protein), lecithin, and cholesterimand salts.

There is a striking contrast between the salts of the corpuscles (cells) and those of the serum, the former consisting chiefly of potassium phosphate, while in the latter sodium chloride (common salt)

8

predominates. In some animals there is *no* sodium chloride in the cells.

This somewhat detailed account of the general chemical composition of blood, which is correct according to the most modern findings,—proves that if the blood cells are taken out of the blood, we have withdrawn a most important group of chemicals, in the absence of which we are not testing *blood* at all.

It is possible, moreover, that the cellular protoplasm—the most complex, baffling, and mysterious substance in the world,—contains many other things about which we know nothing. These, of course, are necessarily absent from the test fluid.

We *are sure*, however, that there is in the protoplasm of our bodies something of which we are in total ignorance, namely, the life-principle. Of the nature of life, its origin, its powers, its reproductive faculty, its ability to feed and sustain itself and the reason and manner of its departure from the cell at the moment of death, we are in profound ignorance. An impenetrable wall meets our attempt to inquire into these abstruse problems.

Let us recall a few important facts. Blood is an ever-changing mixture of solids and liquids, cells and plasma, holding within it from 12 to 20 different chemical substances identical with those found in the dust of the field. These are combined in a most intricate fashion and are controlled by the most elusive and wonderful force known to mankind,—life. Remember that when "blood" tests are made, all the *cells* with their protoplasm and chemicals, are removed; also, the *plasma is changed* by the formation of fibrin, the extraction of which leaves us only a liquid known as serum—a remarkable fluid, but vastly different from original blood, or even plasma.

The serum contains complex proteins (combinations with nitrogen) in two forms,—serum albumen and serum globulins—which probably do not exist side by side in the serum, but are combined to form serum protein,—a very complicated unit.

Professor Ernest R. Starling, M.D., Hon. Sc.D. (Cambridge and Dublin), F.R.C.P., Jodrell, Professor of Physiology, University College, London, in his recent book, "Principles of Human Physiology," writes:

> "The question naturally suggests itself whether in plasma we have not a combination of all its varied collodial constituents to form one labile mass of fluid protoplasm."

The shattering of this combination changes the whole nature of the fluid and invalidates the test. And as we shall see, before we can make *any* tests the combination *must* be broken up by a process of clotting.

The clotting or coagulation of blood is a well-known but complex and little-understood process. As stated in the earlier part of this discussion, it involves the formation of fibrin which enmeshes the blood cells. Clotting ensues whenever blood escapes from its natural habitat—the blood vessels, and undergoes any slight change in the plasma leading to cooling or contact with air or a foreign body. Blood platelets form and then occurs the succession of changes already enumerated.

Starling says:

> "In every case the initiation of the act of clotting would seem to depend on the setting free of thrombokinase in the plasma."

The sole source of thrombokinase is the very perishable formed elements, the platelets, which are probably not found normally in blood. Other substances called antithrombins—which are anti-bodies

10

or antagonizers of fibrin ferment, preventing clotting in circulating blood,—are mentioned by some authorities as constituents of blood.

This brief account of the complex chemistry of the blood demonstrates the highly intricate composition of this life-fluid. We can easily understand how false interpretations can be made from experiments which must be of the greatest delicacy, accuracy and uniformity, and in the performance of which, the slightest alteration or mistake in technique would bring different and conflicting results. It will be proved that the confident and definite conclusions of the evolutionists are logically unjustifiable and in the nature of things impossible.

Before dealing with the actual tests themselves there are a few related phases of this morphological argument which may be briefly mentioned because they have a distant bearing on the whole question.

It is not generally realized how inconstant is the composition of human blood and how great are the differences between the blood from different *human* beings.

Following the work of De Castallo and Sturli, Landstemer and Leimer, Moss and Jansky have shown that all human beings can be divided into four groups, as told by the ability of their blood cells to be dissolved or clumped together (agglutinated) by other human sera, and the ability of their serum to agglutinate other human red cells.

These four groups are characterized as Types 1, 2, 3 and 4. Groups 3 and 4 are about equally common and comprise about eighty-five per cent of all individuals. Group 2 forms about ten per cent and group 1 about five per cent. This "typing" is of immense importance in the operation of transfusing, a valuable treatment for certain diseases, whereby the blood of one individual is introduced into the veins of another. The person who gives the blood is known as the "donor" and the recipient, of course, is the patient.

Group 4 constitutes a universal donor because these cells cannot be agglutinated or damaged by any plasma.

The red cells of Group 1 will agglutinate the serum of Groups 2, 3, and 4, the cells of Group 2 will act on Groups 3 and 4, while Group 3 is incompatible with Groups 2 and 4.

In transfusion, if the wrong types are mixed, very serious, and even fatal, reactions may follow. These reactions, obviously, do not prove that either the donor or the patient is not a member of the Genus Homo, as should be the case if we interpret the result according to the principles adopted by the evolutionist.

The serum of the horse can be used with perfect safety on a human. This does not prove genetic relationship for the horse, nor on the other hand would incompatibility disprove it.

Professor Brumpt found that animals inoculated with the blood of men suffering from sleeping sickness, contracted the disease. The only exceptions were a few apes and pigs. Does this prove a close relationship between these two classes of animals and a separation from other animals and men? No such conclusion can be drawn.

Metchnikoff and other experimenters have tried to develop syphilis in chimpanzees, apes, and monkeys, by inoculating them with a virulent form of the disease, but obtained only very feeble reactions. Does this prove the opposite to the preceding experiment?

All such inferences are absurd and Professor

12

*R*ossle, one of the foremost investigators along this line claims that the blood reaction does not indicate, *nor does it correspond* to the relation existing between any two animals. The facts of comparative anatomy are often in opposition to the findings from the blood.

Between animals and men there are many resemblances but more striking contrasts. As similarity in bodily structure does not prove blood relationship, neither can dissimilarity necessarily be used as proof against such relationship. The mental and spiritual qualities of man separate him by an impassable gulf from all lower animals. This is the real test of heredity and if two individuals have nothing in common in these realms, we can reasonably affirm that they have no "common ancestor."

Again, compare asses' milk and human milk. By adopting the evolutionary logic we would come to some ridiculous conclusions. The qualitative chemical analysis reveals the fact that of all mammals, the ass is closer to man in this respect. We would not dare to insinuate, however, that the latter must class himself with this long-eared fraternity, nor, that because horses' milk is nearest in composition to that of the ass, that we should arrange them in this genetic order from above downward—viz., man, ass, horse, cow.

We come now to the blood tests from which so much is claimed for evolution. Professor Horatio Hackett Newman, Zoologist, University of Chicago, is one of the leading scientists who gave the most extended testimony for evolution at the Scopes trial. His views may be taken to represent the most modern evolutionary view. In the course of his lengthy statement, which covers all the arguments for the theory, he gives considerable prominence to the evidence from blood. In his statement reproduced below, the italics type is inserted to emphasize certain points. Prof. Newman states:—

"The methods of classifying animals just outlined depend upon relatively gross criteria (homologies), as compared with the refinements characteristic of the serological technique used in blood testing. The latter method of classifying animals depends upon chemical similarities and differences in the blood of various animals, and the basic assumption is, once more, that degrees of resemblance parallel degrees of blood relationship. Recent investigation has shown that certain materials in an animal's blood are even more sharply specific than are its visible structural characteristics. Chemical tests of extreme delicacy are used to reveal resemblances in blood. Thus, if we wish to find out what animals are most like man in blood composition, we can find it out in the following manner. *Human blood is drawn and allowed to clot*, a process that *separates the solid materials in the blood from the liquid serum. The latter watery fluid contains the specific human blood ingredients.* Small doses of it are injected at two-day intervals into the blood vessels of a rabbit. At first the rabbit is sickened by the injection, thus showing a marked reaction to the foreign material. In the course of a short time, however, there is no further reaction, and we may conclude that the rabbit is immune. What has happened is that some substance has been developed in the rabbit's blood which neutralizes the toxic effects of human blood. It is a sort of antitoxin and may be

14

spoken of as anti-human serum, a material that may now be used as a delicate indicator of blood kinship. When this anti-human serum is mixed with serum taken from the blood of any human being an immediate and definite white precipitate is formed; when mixed with that of any of the anthropoid apes the precipitate is similar to that formed with human serum, but less abundant reaction and somewhat slower in appearing. The tests showed a less prompt and less abundant reaction with the blood of old world monkeys, a slight but definite reaction with that of new world monkeys, and no noticeable reaction with that of lemurs.

"The tests further indicate that, if strong enough solutions are used and time enough allowed for the 'Precipitate' to settle, there is an unmistakable blood relationship among all mammals, and that degrees of relationship run closely parallel with those based upon homologies. Not only this but not a few affinities, the existence of which had been only vaguely suggested by comparative anatomy, are strongly emphasized by blood tests. One most remarkable revelation is that whales, the most specialized among mammals, are more closely related to the ungulates (hoofed animals), and especially the swine family, than to any of the other groups of the class mammalia,—a diagnosis that had previously been made by several anatomists on what appeared to be slender morphological grounds.

"*At the present time the technique of blood-testing for animal affinities is rather*

15

difficult, and very few workers have attempted to make use of it. The results so far attained, however, are so definite and clean-cut that there is every reason to expect a great future for this type of evolutionary evidence. Many groups of animals have already been tested and, *in general,* the affinities indicated closely parallel those based upon homologies. *There is, however, no exactness about this parallel;* nor could we expect such to be the case; there is no exact parallelism between the teeth and the feet, between the head and the tail. No two systems of an organism exactly keep pace in their evolution; one may remain relatively conservative while the other may become greatly specialized. Of all systems the blood seems to have been the most conservative and to have retained most fully its ancestral characters. It is on this account that blood tests are so valuable in revealing relationships that can scarcely be determined in any other way.

"Far more important than any information as to animal affinities revealed by blood tests is that the classification of animals based on blood tests is essentially the same as that based on morphology . . . the two systems of classification point to the same lines of descent!"

In the first place, we notice the manner of con‌ting the tests, the technique of which he admits ather difficult"; rather! so much so, in fact, that few workers have attempted it.

ay be that the scarcity of workers in this field not only to the inherent difficulties of the

16

tests, but also to the fact that most scientists perceive the obvious impossibility of proving anything from blood-serum. And yet, many who do not place much reliance in it themselves, remain silent when their evolutionist confreres assert themselves so positively. Occasionally, evolutionary ethics are responsible for some strange inconsistencies. Nuttall's experiments are the basis of practically all of the comments by evolutionists. They were performed 21 years ago, and not repeated since, either by him or anyone else. The reason is shown in his own summary of the work, mentioned later in this article.

Notice, then, that "human blood is drawn" into a vessel, "and allowed to clot." This operation, as we have learned, extracts all the solid materials and leaves behind only the fluid portion. But the learned professor goes on to say,—and for all we can tell he is quite serious—"The latter watery fluid contains the specific human blood ingredients."

He must know that this is far from the truth. Think what has been done. The blood cells have all been killed and removed, carrying with them the all-important life principle, and most of all the chemical constituents of blood.

Also, the process of clotting has caused the appearance of "platelets" and new chemicals in different combinations. Yet, notwithstanding this, we are asked to believe that the experimenters are dealing with human "blood." The truth, which cannot be questioned, is that this watery, altered, fluid residue—"serum"—has really very little in common with the original blood. Certainly no individual could live for five minutes if it replaced the normal liquid in the vessels of the body.

When this "serum" is injected into rabbits, horses, apes, monkeys, man, etc., the operation is nothing more than the transference of a solution of certain salts, chiefly table salt, in water. It has a faint resemblance to blood, but is now a poison, or toxin, or "antigen," of which there are many, all having the power of developing in the blood into which they are introduced, a group of substances called "antibodies." In this case the particular "antibody" formed is "preciptin." It causes the throwing-down of a deposit or "precipitate" in the blood of the receptor. Hence this test is known as the "Precipitation" test.

Antibodies are of the nature of antitoxins or antagonizers of toxins or poisons, and in their formation, we are witnessing one of many mysterious phenomena in the functioning of the marvelous defensive mechanism of the body when it is called upon to repel and nullify attacks on it from without.

The Professor writes that "degrees of relationship run closely parallel with those based upon homologies,"—Comparative Anatomy and the like. This too, is not correct, as many authorities acknowledge a number of conflicting results from the different methods of comparison. Newman himself modifies his assertion when he admits, "there is no exactness about this parallel." Then, why mention it at all?

A friend of the writer, Professor Charles Hill-Tout, the well-known anthropologist of Vancouver, B. C., has issued a book, "Man and His Ancestors." It is an attractive and forcible presentation of the subject from the transformist viewpoint. He devotes one entire chapter to this blood-argument, which he considers one of the strongest and most convincing for his theory.

In addition to many unwarranted interpretations of the facts, there are some inaccuracies. He would lead us to infer that the blood cells of all mammals, subjected to "ordinary chemical analysis" reveal practically no differences, a statement which is frequently copied from book to book, and is usually allowed to pass unquestioned by the uninformed reader.

The fact is that most modern textbooks on Physiology, give tables showing marked contrasts between the blood of all mammals and man.

In the 1925 edition of "The Blood," a book written by Professors Gulland and Goodall of the Department of Medicine, University of Edinburgh, chapter eleven is devoted to "The Blood in Certain Animals."

In this chapter, a table is given which compares the blood of fifteen mammals, and great dissimilarities are shown in the number and proportions of the various cellular elements, both when compared with one another and with man.

Another table reveals great differences in the size of the cells, and in their staining qualities, explained by the variation in chemical compositions of their protoplasm.

In their discussion of "Haemophilia," a disease of the blood marked by diminished clotting power, and in which there is danger of serious and even fatal hemorrhage from a slight cut, they mention a well-known fact under "Treatment." It is this,—the blood serum of rabbits may be injected, with very favorable and curative results, into the human patient, but ox-serum causes severe and dangerous symptoms. What is the significance, if any, of this peculiar fact?

The rabbit belongs to the family of Rodents, which, according to evolutionary Zoology, is just above the Insectivora, and below the Ungulata or Hoofed Mammals. The Rodents include rats, mice, squirrels, porcupines, rabbits, etc. Four groups are recognized, of which the squirrels, porcupines, rats

19

and rabbits serve as types. The rabbit group includes hares, rabbits, and picas.

The next group above rabbits are the Ungulata, of which there are two sub-divisions, Perissodactyls or Odd-Toed, and Artiodactyls, or Even-Toed Hoofed Mammals. Of course, different "common ancestors" are assumed because of the wide gaps between animals like the horse and rhinoceros, or pig and hippopotamus.

The other Artiodactyls is made up of non-ruminants (pigs, peccaries and hippopotami), and the much larger group of ruminants (cud-chewers), giraffes, deer, antelopes, sheep and cattle. The last two are considered the "highest and most progressive."

And yet, strange to say, the blood serum of the ox, which, according to the theory, is much nearer to man than the rabbit, is poison to man, while the serum of the rabbit, a million or more years removed from man,—again according to the theory,—is entirely compatible with human serum and shows a much more marked resemblance in chemical composition.

What conclusions are we to draw as to the value of the elaborate and exact (?) classification of animals, constantly presented by the evolutionist and based on the serum test? The multitude of inexplicable contradictions renders this classification absolutely without meaning to the critical and intelligent student.

Most writers on blood confess to an immense ignorance concerning this baffling, complex solution of living cells and chemicals, and readily admit that all opinions on its chemistry, comparing man with man, and especially man with other mammalians, are certain to be erroneous because of our lack of knowledge and the inherent impossibility of governing the conditions of the tests.

Even with the most meticulous care as to technique, the experimenters are unable to prevent variations and mistakes. Blood is so exceedingly sensitive and so instantaneously responsive to the slightest change in environment leading to cooling or to foreign contact, and so subject to constant alteration from the countless complex food-products which are being introduced into it, that no two specimens, even in the same individual, are ever identical.

How, then, can we expect any fixed chemical composition in a fluid of this character, and how can there be any finality or exactitude to analytical tests?

As the basis of his enthusiastic acclaim, Professor Hill-Tout uses the 16,000 tests and tabulated results of Dr. George Nuttall of Cambridge University. He states that these results have been confirmed by other independent workers and are "well-established facts of science." He does not seem to have grasped the extreme delicacy and liability to error in these experiments as Professor Newman has. These tests are now two decades old so they are not in any sense recent as might be inferred. There's a reason for their long neglect and present revival.

Six tables of Nuttall's are given, purporting to prove the conclusive character of this kind of evidence for evolution. Ignoring for the moment, the undisputed fact that these figures are open to grave suspicion because of their utter impossibility of avoiding error, and forgetting that Nuttall was not using "blood," but "serum,"—we still find some curious and striking discrepancies in the figures offered as "evidence" of relationship between man and the lower animals.

In Table "A," Anti-Human Precipitation Serum is tested against the blood of Men, Old World

21

Monkeys, New World Monkeys, Marmosets, and Lemurs. The results indicate that Old World Monkeys, (O. W. M.) are 8 points removed from man, while New World Monkeys, (N. W.M.) are 22 points distant.

But Table B shows O.W.M. 35 points away from Man and Anthropoids, a discrepancy of 27 degrees, between the two tables.

Table C proves O. W. M., Man and Anthropoids to be practically identical.

Table D gives 13 points between O. W. M. and Man, and 27 points between Man and Anthropoids.

Table D, to add to our confusion, suggests that Man is a real Ape, as Friedenthal once claimed. Also, he seems to be a Monkey,—Old World Species. Well may we ask,—"What is man anyhow?"

Table C reveals the fact that O. W. M. and N. W. M. are 42 points separated, but in Table D, an impassable gulf of 64 degrees yawns between.

Table A does not permit Marmoset and O. W. M. to come closer together than 42 points, but Table D increases the distance to 64.

In Table E, Anti-sheep serum was used on horses and other animals. According to one test, horse and sheep are 84 degrees removed. In this same table, where anti-pig serum was used against horses and sheep, the two latter animals are close brothers, only 3 points apart.

In Table E, also, using the first method, pig and horse seem to be about the same kind of animal,—20 and 16, but in the next method, there looms an unbridgable chasm of 74 points.

In the one, sheep and dog are widely separated by 93 points, while in the other, they are identical with 13 points to the credit.

Table F purports to reveal the generic relation-

22

ship of various groups of animals. Here anti-monkey serum was injected into 12 different kinds,—cheiroptera (long-fingered bats), ungulata (hoofed animals, horse, cow, etc.), carnivora (dogs, cats, weasels, etc.). The conclusion we must draw seems to be that only 3 classes of these mammals bear any resemblance to monkeys, these being horse, dog and kangaroo. The last-named is closest, the dog next, and the horse at the furthest extremity in the ratio of 8, 2, 1.

This unquestionably teaches us,—if it teaches anything—that the blood, either of the kangaroo or dog, is safer to man than that of the horse. If the worker experiments with himself according to this principle, it is probable that he would not live long enough to record his experience.

Yet we are informed with the greatest positiveness that the reactions invariably indicate the genetic relationship, and agree absolutely with other methods of comparison.

Nuttall also gives the results of Quantitative Tests (pp. 3, 9, 320 etc.), in which he measured the amount of precipitum as deposit produced by the various blood tested.

There are some results so exceedingly peculiar not to say absurd, that it is difficult to see how any conclusions of value can be drawn.

In the first tests, jackal, otter, ox, sheep, antelope and Tibetan bear, show a definite relationship to man.

In the second and third tests one species of baboon is as closely related to man, and a short-tailed Old World Monkey (Macacus Rhesus) more closely related, than the ape.

In another test in which the actual proportion of deposit is given very exactly in decimals, ox, sheep and baboon are grouped together with .004; and the whale-bone whale, one species of baboon, the tiger, the African antelope and MAN are the same,— .003. Accordingly, we may make our choice of ancestors between whale, antelope, tiger and baboon!

But we have other possible choices. In the second test, man, the civit cat, and the tenrec, a little mammal of Madagascar, are all on the same level .001. Our forebears are numerous if not noble!

These tests certainly seem to prove rather more than Professor Nuttall bargained for! Even Professor A. B. Scott, friendly as he would like to be to the evidence for evolution has to admit: "It could hardly be maintained than an ostrich and a parrot are more nearly allied than a wolf and a hyena, and yet that would be the inference from the blood tests."

What kind of intellectual equipment and discrimination must we have in order to draw such inferences from the jumbled mass of contradictions and inconsistencies provided by these absurd "tests"?

In his "Berlin Discussion of Evolution," Eric Wasmann most emphatically refutes a number of these confident claims for blood. He writes in regard to the alleged proofs from these same 16,000 experiments of Nuttall:

> "Investigations into the reaction of the blood, have been made by Friedenthal, Nuttall, Uhlenhuth, Wasserman, Schutze and others, in some cases with the express intention of tracing the relation between man and the higher apes, in others for various purposes. Some years ago Dr. Friedenthal published a work in which he declared, as the result of his researches into the action of the blood, that man was not only descended from the apes, but was a genuine ape himself. This

24

conclusion is deducted from the following facts. It is ascertained that if the blood from one class of vertebrates, especially of mammals, be injected into the veins of another animal, symptoms of disease appear, in consequence of the decomposition of the red corpuscles of one kind of blood by the serum of the other. There is, however, no such result when the two kinds of animals are closely related. Carefully experiments have proved that there is a very feeble reaction between human blood and that of apes, and this has led to the inference that man and the apes must be closely connected. Conversely, in the reaction of the anti-serum, the morbid effect is most marked in the case of animals most closely related.

"But we are not justified in regarding a chemical and physiological resemblance as constituting a blood relationship in the sense of having common origin. Let us assume that there is a blood resemblance between the blood of apes and that of man. This would prove that the same kind of likeness exists in the blood of men and apes, as in their skeletons and other organs, but similarity does not imply blood-relationship, such as exists between cousins and kinfolk. Rossle has recently brought out an interesting work on this subject (in the Biologisches Zentralblatt for 1905, Nos. 11 and 12.) He is of the opinion that the blood reaction only enables us to say that one animal is more closely related to another than to a third, but it does not show *how closely* related, still less that man ought to be classed with the higher apes.

25

He (Rossle) also insists upon the fact that the chemical composition of the fluids of the body, such as the blood, is no more constant, for instance, than the formation of the skeleton, therefore, evidence based on resemblance of the blood is no more trustworthy, in support of a common descent, than that based on similarities of the skeleton and other morphological resemblances.

"And the blood reaction points to a close relation between creatures that are morphologically far apart. It would seem that we cannot make much of evidence derived from similarity of blood if comparative morphology arrives at different results.

"More recent investigations by Uhlenhuth and Friedenthal tend to throw doubt upon the alleged actual existence of similarity between human blood and that of higher apes, and this circumstance renders untenable all the conclusions based on the similarity, viz., that man is closely related to the higher apes or is even an ape himself.

"I would like to refer to some recent microscopical investigations made by Raehlmann into the red corpuscles. Those occurring in human blood present certain peculiarities that are not found in the blood of other vertebrates."

On page 299 of the same book, Wasmann writes

"I was very glad to hear Dr. Friedenthal state definitely that his chief aim was simply to demonstrate the chemical and physiological resemblances existing between different kinds of blood. We are therefore of one mind, and the popular idea that he interpreted kin-

26

ship of blood to imply a common origin or descent was based upon a misconception."

All the facts enumerated should now enable us to get at the meat in the cocoanut. What value, if any, have these 16,000 tests of Nuttall? Do they prove anything more than a chemical resemblance between the different kinds of blood?

A general survey of this work reveals grave and obvious fallacies which render conclusions absolutely valueless, and shows that there are very slight grounds indeed for the confident expressions of the animal-ancestry advocates.

Professor Nuttall seems to realize the difficulties inherent in the experiments, when he writes:

"In view of the crudity of our methods, it is not surprising if certain discrepancies may be encountered in the course of investigations conducted by biological methods. The object of my investigation has been to determine certain broad facts with regard to blood affinities, consequently my studies must be regarded in the light of a preliminary investigation which will have to be continued along special lines by many workers in the future."

In his book, he devotes fifteen pages to "Sources of Error," showing how great is the risk of mistakes which invalidate every conclusion.

We must remember that neither Professor Nuttall nor any of the workers used "blood" in their tests. It was simply the chemically changed liquid residue left after the process of clotting had been completed.

Not even were they working with normal blood plasma since from this, many valuable constituents have been extracted and another new substance added in the process of formation of "platelets." And of course, all the blood cells with their amazingly complex quota of chemical substances upon which known life-principle had been completely eliminated.

Under such conditions as these, it would seem to require only a very ordinary degree of intelligence to reject any conclusions whatever as to blood kinship, derived from these operations.

Think of the question in this way. These blood cells are living individuals, breathing, feeding, excreting and moving, almost the same as any other living organisms. They live and reproduce in a liquid environment which surrounds them and supplies them with the necessities of life, air, water and food. Humans do the same, except that our environment is not fluid and we adopt different means of securing these three essentials to life.

What has the experimenter done? He kills these little cellular individuals, and then proceeds to examine their environment, the watery liquid with its complex quota of chemical substances upon which the minute creatures depend for their existence.

From investigations which are very difficult, uncertain and tricky, he proposes to decide the relationship between the many dead owners of the blood, which in life, contained the same basic elements in varied combinations.

Could we not, just as logically, apply the same principle in a slightly modified form? With equal promise of accurate results we might exterminate a collection of representatives of Genus Homo, preferably perhaps, Fundamentalists from benighted Tennessee! Also some salt water fish, a number of fresh water fish, kangaroos from Australia, and Hippopotami from Africa, Rhinoceros from India, Camels from Central Asia, and Llamas from South America? Having extinguished the life of these animals, we proceed to investigate their environment,

28

the atmosphere they have breathed, the liquids they have absorbed and the essential foods they have consumed.

After a very careful analysis, we prepare a number of tables supposed to give the exact genetic relationship between the dead animals and man, the latter represented by the unfortunate citizens of the Southern State, once dwellers in that region of medieval darkness. Who can deny that our tabulated results would have as much claim to accuracy and dependability as those of Nuttall, "et al"?

What, then, is the explanation of blood resemblances and differences? The blood-serum is nothing more than a phase of the morphological argument, which compares the structure of various animals, and from the assembled similarities and dissimilarities, affects to prove a common origin or a different origin.

There is one good and sufficient answer to all such alleged "proof," and it is, that similarity in bodily structure and formation is absolutely no evidence of a genetic blood relationship.

If there is anything in the statement that blood-reaction reveals the measure of kinship, why should one human being thrive on blood, which, if injected into another human being, would result in death to the second?

Again, why should the blood of a horse introduced into a man's veins, be less harmful than the blood of another human being injected into the same man? Is one of these men, on account of this peculiarity, to be excluded from membership in the human race, while the horse is granted honorable admission?

God created different kinds of mammals. For their preservation and existence, He gave them blood. It varies somewhat in different types, the variation

29

depending on conditions of which we are in almost complete ignorance. But why should this give us the right to assume a "common ancestor" for all?

It would seem to be the most sensible and natural thing in the world for an Omniscient and Omnipotent Creator and Designer to provide a similar circulating, nourishing, fluid medium to flow through the vessels of all animal bodies. While the constituents of this medium are the same in their simplest form, their combinations are subject to innumerable changes, incidental and inevitable because of the great variety of foods constantly thrown into the blood stream.

Each animal, no matter how widely separated genetically, has to perform the same functions of respiration, digestion, excretion, movement, all of these accompanying and necessary to life. The same or similar organs and tissues are the logical outcome of perfection in the general basic plan.

The Creator's plan for this intricate and involved life system, as we see it in the whole animal kingdom around us, the members, interwoven and interdependent, related and unrelated, demands many complicated similarities and dissimilarities. Such a vast number of individual types makes it manifestly impossible that there should *not* be many instances of similar or even identical structure in forms widely separated from each other,—considered on any rational basis of classification.

The blood is only one of the many tissues like bones, muscles and organs, and a similarity in blood composition between man and lower animals, even if much more marked than it actually is, would have little or no bearing as evidence of community of origin, or of an evolutionary process connecting man with inferior life-forms.

Were it possible, by careful juggling of the peculiar necessary conditions, to establish *close* resemblance between the blood of the higher ape and man, the problem would still be the same.

As frequently happens, there is confusion of thought regarding two ideas, namely, resemblances in the chemical properties of two kinds of blood, and identity of genetic relationship.

Unless and until we are absolutely *certain* that blood from two animals cannot be chemically similar without having a common ancestry we have no right to draw the latter inference. Without doubt, no such *certainty* has been proven to exist.

The propounders of this blood argument have extracted from the facts, not the evidence which the facts proclaim, but the interpretation of their own highly cultured imagination, dominated by a materialistic and evolutionary bias.

Parallelism in organisms having separate ancestors, arises, not from heredity, but from the uniform action of universal morphogenetic forces. Organisms have much in common that transcends any possible scheme of evolution, much that cannot be brought into alignment with the position arbitrarily assigned them in the evolutionary family tree.

Living matter has certain universal properties, pro-governed by distinct laws of organization quite adequate to account for all observed homologies and analogies.

Exposed to similar environmental conditions, organisms have the power of solving their individual life-problems in parallel fashion, irrespective of any near or remote relationship.

A logical, intensive and critical examination of all the evidence, affords no justification for interpreting the resemblance of homology—of which this blood similarity is one—as surviving vestiges of an ancient hypothetical "common-ancestral" type.

OTHER BOOKS BY DR. BROWN

GOD'S MASTERPIECE...Man's Body. 352 Pages. $2.50
MIRACLES OF SCIENCE—287 Pages $2.00
FOOTPRINTS OF GOD—246 Pages $2.00
I WILL COME AGAIN—115 Pages............$1.25
GOD AND YOU—141 Pages $1.25
MEN, MONKEYS, AND MISSING LINKS ...... .25
EVOLUTION and The Blood Precipitation Test.. .25
MUST YOUNG PEOPLE Believe in Evolution.. .25
GOD'S CREATIVE FORETHOUGHT .... .35

God's Creative Forethought

by

ARTHUR I. BROWN

M. D. C. M., F. R. C. S. E.

Author of

Evolution and the Blood-Precipitation Test
Men, Monkeys and Missing Links
Evolution and the Bible
The Acid-Test of Evolution
Etc.

PUBLISHED BY
RESEARCH SCIENCE BUREAU, INC.
5141 Angeles Mesa Drive
Los Angeles, Calif.

GOD'S CREATIVE FORETHOUGHT

There is being conducted today a very determined, well-organized, and extensive propaganda, the purpose of which is, as the utterances of those behind the movement express it, to "rid the world of the absurd idea of a personal God."

In October, 1925, there was incorporated in the city of New York by Supreme Court Judge Ford, The American Society for the Advancement of Atheism. This organization through its president, Charles Smith, frankly calls itself a wrecking society. They intend to destroy the Church, the clergy, and those fundamentals of the Christian faith upon which Christianity is founded. The Bible is speedily to become a forgotten Book,—in fact, these agitators tell us that they intend to see that it shall be taken from us..

They have small regard for the Person of Jesus Christ. Many of their number affirm that no such Person ever lived. Those who grudgingly give assent to the existence of Jesus of Nazareth, charge that He was a mental and moral degenerate. They, of course, ridicule the idea of an Infallible Bible, of Sin, the Fall of Man, of Redemption, of the Deity of Christ, and all other basic doctrines which have been the foundation of our faith.

It looks like an impossible task for them to carry out their wrecking program according to schedule, but they count, and not without reason, on the apathy of believing Christians, and on the great inroads which Modernism has made on the tenets of orthodoxy.

It is well frequently to remind ourselves of the abundant and irrefutable evidence everywhere around us, of the loving forethought of God, the Creator, in bringing into being all the innumerable wonders of earth, sea and sky. These show indisputably, that design is constantly to be seen. If there is design, there must of necessity be a Designer behind the design. If it can be proved that there is a personal God, the arguments of the atheist become weak and foolish.

To the orthodox Christian, our God is a loving Father, interested in the welfare and happiness of His children whom He has created. We believe we have seen many undoubted evidences that He has thought and planned for us. When the work of creation was planned in His infinite mind, He determined that the climax of all His creative activites should be man, for him everything was made "that is made."

The 19th Psalm tells us that "the heavens declare the glory of God, and the firmament showeth His handiwork." The created universe testifies to the glory of Him who made sun, moon and stars, as He scattered into the depths of illimitable space all the countless myriads of heavenly worlds, from His omnipotent hand. He gave these worlds their exact orbits in which they were to travel, and beyond the bounds of which they were forbidden to go.

The earth on which man is found, is one of the smallest orbs in the skies, yet here it has pleased God in His infinite wisdom, to work out an inconceivably amazing plan for the redemption of a lost and sinning race of humans. Whether life as we know it, exists on any other planet or not, a study of the conditions surrounding the earth, seems to show that these conditions are not the result of chance but of design.

As a very humble unit of the solar system, our world is dependent on the sun for heat and light, without which life would be impossible. The earth is distant from the sun approximately 92,000,000 miles. Is there any significance in this distance? If we were 192,000,000 miles away from our source of heat, we should be all frozen to death speedily. If we were much nearer than at present, we should be consumed with the solar radiations. We find ourselves, fortunately, at just the right place in space in order to derive the necessary heat to sustain life.

The earth revolves on its axis once in twenty-four hours, giving us 12 hours day and 12 hours night. This proportion has been proved just what mankind needs. The darkness is as necessary as the light. Too much darkness, or too much light alike would be fatal. How does it come that this rate of motion on its axis happens to be exactly suited to our requirements, unless it has been so planned? Can it be chance?

Our movement around the sun is completed in 365 days, 9 hours, 6 minutes, and 6 seconds. The seasons pass in regular rotation, spring, summer, autumn, winter, their length caused by our speed of motion along this solar path. How is this, unless God is responsible?

The earth is not vertical but is tipped at an angle of $23\frac{1}{2}$ to the ecliptic. This strange position is responsible for our climatic conditions. How was the earth given this peculiar tilt?

Again, how are the planets and innumerable suns and stars in space kept moving at an incredible but uniform rate of speed, if not held in the grip of some Omnipotent Hand? The question asked by God of Job,—"Canst thou bind the sweet influences of Pleiades?" solves the problem for the devout believer. The even influence of this great group of seven stars, controls the movements of the entire solar system. The Infinite Intelligence which commands this mighty power is the Eternal Jehovah.

Inert matter is made up of some seventy odd elements which exist alone or in various combinations with one another. All the material things on earth are built of a few primary building materials. Atoms and electrons are the smallest conceivable portions of matter, and these few different kinds, can, by their countless compounds, be changed into a multitude of apparently unlike forms. And yet each atom is subject to definite and unvarying laws. In every chemical compound the kinds and relative quantities of the constituent elements are fixed and invariable. Each molecule of water must always contain two atoms of hydrogen and one atom of oxygen. It can have no other composition. This same principle is seen with every other compound in nature. Thirty-two pounds of sulphur, for instance, must have fifty-six pounds of iron with which to unite. Less iron would leave some sulphur untouched, more iron would mean that a portion of the latter would not enter into combination with the sulphur. And so with all elements. Can this be blind chance, or is it the product of Infinite Wisdom?

Some elements are poisonous, others quite harmless. But, the various poisonous elements exist in such small quantities that they are all locked up in harmless and useful compounds. In fact, many of the most useful compounds contain elements which, if uncombined, would be destructive to life. This is true of one of the greatest blessings and necessities of life, common table salt, which is composed of two deadly substances, sodium and clorine.

Why is it that the deadly chlorine gas is not as

plentiful as Oxygen? Phosphorous is another element which would spread death and destruction in its wake, but it is absolutely necessary to the organic world. It is found in great abundance in the seeds of plants and the bones of animals, and in all fertile soils. But the form in which it is combined, phosphates, makes it perfectly safe and adapted to its designed use.

If the earth is to be stable and to remain permanently above the water of the oceans, then most of the minerals on the surface of the earth must be in combinations which will not dissolve in water, otherwise all land would soon be carried in solution into the seas. This peculiar kind of combination has been well accomplished by the great preponderance of a few elements, like silicon, aluminum, calcium, magnesium, iron, carbon, oxygen and others, which unite in harmless, insoluble compounds, giving permanence to the continents, and also forming proper soils for the growth of plants. What Law governs all this?

Without water there would be no life, and with this substance, the Creator did some amazing things. It is made up with two gases, hydrogen and oxygen. Hydrogen is the most inflammable gas known, and oxygen is necessary to all combustion. But when God combined these two, He made something which will extinguish all the fires of earth if it be in sufficient quantity.

Water is the home of countless myriads of God's creatures, and in order to preserve their lives, He was compelled to break a law of physics, which holds in regard to all other liquids. When liquids are subjected to cold they invariably condense, become heavier and sink. But while this is true of water when cooled to $4°$ C, at that point the law is broken and from that degree of cold to 0° C, or freezing, water expands and becomes lighter, so that it rises to the surface. If this were not the case, in winter the rivers and lakes would freeze, and ice being heavier, would sink to the bottom so that, soon, if the cold were sufficiently intense, the streams would be solid masses of ice. This would mean death to all the fish. But instead of killing them, ice becomes a beautiful protective covering for the myriads of creatures living beneath it.

Mankind breathes air which has a definite composition being made up of 21 parts oxygen and 79 parts of nitrogen, the latter acting as a dilutent. The question arises as to the reason for this invariable proportion, so excellently suited to the requirements of the race. If the amount of oxygen had been greatly increased the perils to property and to human life would have been tremendously increased, because of the destructive effect of conflagrations. Cities could not exist as fires could never be put out. If the nitrogen were increased in amount, combustion and breathing would be impossible and life would become extinct. Is this the result of chance also?

This air which we breathe so easily is found to contain a large amount of watery vapor, estimated at more than 50,000,000 tons. It is an interesting observation to know that without this water, life would be impossible. Its presence retains the sun's heat during the hours of the night when it is gradually given up. If it were not found in this proportion, no matter how hot it might be in the day, before morning arrived the temperature would be, possibly 30° or 40° below zero. Does this not look as if a designing Intelligence had something to do with it?

Earth dwellers are bearing an air pressure of 15

pounds to the square inch from an atmosphere which extends up 45 or 50 miles. It is only of comparatively recent date that this knowledge was gained. Formerly it was not known that the air had weight, but away back in the time of Job we read that "God gave to the winds their weight." How did this scientific statement find its way into the Bible so many centuries ago unless God, the Master Scientist of the universe put it there? And why this exact pressure of 15 pounds? This happens to be exactly suited to our capacity and our need. Is it mere chance?

There is an interesting relation between inanimate matter, and plants and animals. The Genesis Record affirms that matter came first, then vegetables, then animals. It is strange that the human writer should get this order just right unless he had an Informant. We now know that all flesh is made from about 16 elements, which are identically the same as those found in the dust beneath our feet. Vegetables are able to absorb and derive sustenance from these lifeless chemicals. Animals cannot do that but must live off the plants, while man has both for his food. The Creator is the great Economist and nothing in Nature is ever wasted. One of the products of the combustion of plants is oxygen, which is necessary to man, but man excretes through the lungs a poisonous gas which, unless somehow consumed, would endanger life. At this point the plants enter and eagerly take up the Carbonic Acid gas which to them is food. This remarkable adaptation would seem to point to a carefully worked out plan. But, a plan never makes itself!

When plants and animals decay, they give back to the air and soil the material of which they are composed, usually in such forms as to provide food for the

—8—

plants. So, the same matter may enter, again and again, into the constitution of countless individuals.

Many flowers are dependent for their fertilization on certain insects, while many of the latter are equally dependent on the plant for their continuing life. The insects seem to be infallibly guided by an unseen Intelligence as they carry out their destined duties, not knowing how or why. Surely a multitude of these wonderful adaptations point unerringly to a Supreme Power.

Can it be imagined that all the gorgeous beauties of sky and sunset, of cloud and evening star, have come from blind chance? Can evolution account for the rich and amazing colorings of flower, insect and animal? How account for mind, and spirit, and the universal instinct to worship the Unknown, qualities which man alone of all creatures possesses?

The animal kingdom presents many remarkable instances of design. Certain animals possess powers which cannot be accounted for by any known evolutionary process. The surprising instincts which animals possess are necessary to the life of the animal. Without them they would speedily die. Evolution affirms that these powers have been developed gradually through millions of years. That is, there must have been a period in the life of the animal when it was without that which is now indispensable to it. How then, may we ask, could the individual sustain itself? It must inevitably have died, and with it, the entire species would have been obliterated. The first animals then must have had the powers of modern relatives. If that is true, these powers or instincts must have been conferred upon them by the Creator. How else could they acquire them?

In the vicinity of the island of Fiji, there lives an

annelid worm known as the palolo. This little denizen of the Pacific Ocean lives about six feet below the surface of the water, and attaches itself to the coral rock, never leaving this submarine home for the entire period of its existence, which is one year.

Sharp on the stroke of midnight at the last quarter of the October moon, each year, it suddenly loosens itself from its hold on the rock, and with countless millions of its fellows, rises to the surface in order to engage in the act of reproducing a new palolo. This is accomplished by the process of budding or the appearance of slight protuberances from the outside of the body, the process taking from midnight to 8 o'clock in the morning, when the new individual is complete and sinks down to attach itself to the same old rock.

The natives know when this event is to transpire because the little annelid worm keeps astronomical time, and is never ahead or behind schedule. The fishermen and ready with their nets and a good catch of this edible sea-dweller is always assured.

Where does this palolo keep its alarm clock, and who taught it to know when midnight strikes? Can evolution possibly explain such an amazing performance? The only satisfying solution is that God gave the knowledge to this creature of His.

A tiny aquarium fish, phyrrilhima filamentosa, exhibits a very reamarkable series of actions which require some explaining by the materialist. This fish having laid its egg, is not satisfied that the bottom of the bowl is a safe place to rear its young, so proceeds to deposit the egg above the surface of the water about one and a half or two inches, on the side of the glass.

—10—

Knowing apparently, that this egg must be kept moist otherwise it will surely dry up and die, it adopts a most ingenious method of accomplishing this object. As it swims about, constantly on the move, it gives its little tail a vigorous but very accurate flip which results in a drop of water being deposited on the egg. With great precision it repeats this act every few seconds, keeping up the performance for about four days when the egg hatches out and baby fish slides down the side where it is warmly welcomed by the fond mother.

Who taught this little animal the knowledge necessary for this amazing series of actions, all apparently the results of intelligence? Evolution, certainly can not be given the credit. No—the Intelligence responsible for this, is the intelligence of the Creator who, at the moment of creation, gave this marvellous instinct to His creature.

Another little creature which offers an insoluble puzzle to the materialist is a certain variety of wasp that performs some wonderful feats, in its ordinary routine of work for its unborn children. This wasp builds its home underground by laboriously excavating a few rooms, perhaps three of four, in itself an almost herculean task, when one considers that the work consists of carrying tiny grains of sand and dirt up through the special opening provided with a trap-door arrangement so as to provide safety and privacy for the busy mother.

This devoted parent knows that its tiny offspring, when hatched, must have, for its food supply, living meat! Nothing else will be accepted, and this curious appetite presents a formidable problem for the wasp to solve. But while preparing the home for its babies whom it is destined never to see, it has not forgotten

—11—

to look for the proper rations, and on a neighboring vine, in the person of one or more fat and succulent caterpillars, they are found.

When the hidden rooms are completely ready, the wasp is confronted with a most delicate surgical operation, requiring a precise knowledge of anatomy and the possession of inconceivable surgical skill, along with the necessary tool of the most delicate description. The caterpillar must be completely and instantly paralyzed, but not killed, by the very first attack. The attacker goes up to the unsuspecting caterpillar and with a lightning-like thrust of its tiny lance, penetrates one of the nine ventral ganglia, or nerve centres which are to be found along the abdominal wall of the crawling victim. These nerve-centres are only of microscopic size, and the anatomical instinct, and operative skill which enables it to make helpless its helpless opponent at the first stroke, is, in many ways, one of the most striking phenomena in all nature. Not content with one sword-thrust, it proceeds to puncture the remaining eight ganglia, until there is scarcely a movement visible. Then the living meat must be transported to the distant home, necessitating the exhibition of amazing strength, as the little insect tugs, pulls, and pushes the caterpiller along home. When it is safely dropped into the room where it is to be needed, the mother wasp displays another bit of inexplicable wisdom.

The head of the caterpillar contains, of course, the vital organs, which, if eaten, would immediately result in the death of the necessary food, and the consequent annihiliation of the infant wasp. The mother, apparently sensing this important fact, never lays its egg on the head but always back on the tail end. In due course, after the mother has departed, leaving the egg to bring forth the baby it will never see, the larval wasp is hatched, and finding its food directly beneath it, takes an ample bite of the caterpillar, still living but helpless, and when the entire immature butterfly is consumed, the larva or worm which is to develop into the fully-developed wasp, goes into the next or pupa stage of its life history, all its wants having been supplied by the splendid work of its unknown mother.

Is it possible to conceive of these wonderful powers as the product of any evolutionary process? In that case, there was a time when the mother wasp knew nothing of anatomy or surgery. If that is true, what would become of the wasp when it attempted to paralyze its meat supply? There is but one answer. The wasp would be killed and the entire race of wasps would be annihilated, so that today there would be no such wasp family to be found. We are compelled to believe that the first wasp knew as much as its modern descendents, and possessed a knowledge which must have been conferred by an Omniscient Maker.

The story of the Hive Bee (Apis) gives us another illustration of the astonishing powers of insect life. When spring reawakens the sleeping earth, and the willow trees are putting on their new garments, and violet and primrose send out invitations rich with fragrance, the bee-world resumes its busy life.

The first job is to institute the usual spring cleaning of the hive and to build new combs of hexagonal or six-sided cells to accomodate the eggs the queen has already begun to lay. The workers are hard at different kinds of work, some bringing in fresh stores of pollen and honey, while others are in charge of the fast-filling nurseries.

The queen is the head of the community, not because her wits are superior, for in reality her daughters far surpass her in brains and activity, but solely because she alone has the egg-laying power and so is able to increase or restore the population. Egg-laying is her only work, all her wants being supplied by her faithful attendants.

These attendants are the worker-bees who sustain the life of the hive. They are active, intelligent, but sterile females, their reproductive organs being undeveloped. The amazing powers of these bees are among the most astonishing in all nature.

The third section of the bee community is that of the drones or males, which take no part in the work but forage only for themselves, and even then are not able to satisfy thoroughly their greed for honey. They spend much time in flying around, very energetically looking for an emerging queen, in which hope they are usually disappointed.

The diligence of the working bees is immense. They toil from morning to night, with ceaseless energy gathering precious stores of honey and pollen. In the summer-time the average life of a worker bee is said to be only about two months. It literally works itself to death. It has been calculated that in a colony of 50,000 bees, there are 30,000 workers, which, making on an average of ten trips a day will visit 300,000 flowers. About 37,000 loads of nectar are required for the production of a pound of honey.

When a flower is visited, the bee protrudes its tongue into the flower tube, sucking the nectar into its mouth, and thence into the "honey bag," where it is manufactured into honey. How this is done is a mystery which human ingenuity cannot fathom, because no human skill has been able to make honey from the sweet tasting watery fluid called nectar.

The golden pollen which the bee collects as it innocently rubs its body against the precious powder when it enters the flower, is kneaded into a little ball and carried carefully back to the hive in the "pollen-basket," a curious little cavity in the bee's hind leg. This cavity is made possible by the peculiar arrangement of the hairs on the leg.

The bees' comb made up of hexagonal cells, is one of the wonders of the world. The cells are made of thin plates of pliable wax, which comes from little pockets or manufacturing centres on the bee's abdomen. In order to start the secretion of the wax, great heat is needed, so the bees gather together in a great pendant mass, their wings buzzing rapidly all the while. Presently, "a strange sweat, white as snow and airier than the down of a wing, is beginning to break over the swarm." These wax scales are removed by the worker bees with a pair of pincers found at one of her knee-joints, and then chewed into a soft paste which can be moulded into the delicate fabric of the cells.

This comb, notwithstanding its extraordinary fragility, about one one hundred and eightieth of an inch in thickness, is able to suspend a weight thirty times as great as its own. A small block of wax is attached to the roof of the hive, and serves as foundation, from which the layers of cells grow out downwards and sideways, always leaving a gangway for the streams of bees to pass to and fro.

The shape of the cell, six-sided, is exceedingly well adapted to accommodate the body of the grub, and also is devised to prevent waste, although when occasion requires it, in odd corners, triangular, square or other shaped cells are constructed. The measurements in a typical cell are geometrically accurate, the worker achieving a precision which baffles description.

The cells are not placed horizontally, but are given a slight upward tilt, which prevents the spilling of thin honey from the tissue-like paper walls of the cell. Cells are always filled to the brim before being capped. These astonishing measurements, let it be remembered, are all taken in absolute darkness, which fact makes the wonder greater still.

A luckless mouse sometimes ventures into the hive where it is speedily stung to death by the enraged colony. Now, on the floor of their dwelling, they find a dead body, which will soon become a source of offense to the hive. The body is too heavy to be carried out, yet it must not be allowed to remain in its present dangerous position. Bees have the power to manufacture, not only honey, bee-bread, and wax, but also a substance called propolis, which is virtually a very efficient varnish. This is now called into play and thousands of bees swarm over the corpse and cover every portion of it carefully with the varnish so that when the operation is concluded, they have sealed up the dead mouse in an air-tight tomb, where it will gradually go back into its primordial dust.

The bee nurseries are interesting. Within the hive, the younger workers are always busily looking after the newborn, and attending on the queen. The newly hatched grubs are fed on a kind of pap regurgitated by the nurses from their stomachs, but in a day or two, the food is strengthened by the addition of pollen bread, and later with honey. Then the larvae spin cocoons and the workers shut the cells with little caps of porous wax. Within these walls they rest for 13 days, after which yet another generation of worker bees bite off the roofs of their cradles, and prepare to participate in the hive's busy life.

The drone cells in which the queen deposits unfertilized cells are larger than the ordinary cell, and later in the season when princess bees are being planned for, still larger cells are built, as a mark of respect to their future queen. The lying-in room must be of special size. In these "royal" cells, the queen lays the usual fertilized eggs, which in the ordinary way, would develop into sterile undeveloped female bees. But, when the grubs from these cells hatch out, they are fed upon a peculiar food, "royal jelly," direct from the mouths of their attendants, instead of the usual fare of masticated pollen. The surprising effect of this special diet is to make the grubs develop into "princesses" with fully developed female organs, instead of into workers. What the nature of this food is, no one knows.

How does the bee come by these powers? Her instincts are necessary for the propagation of the species and the life and welfare of the hive. If, as evolutionists affirm, instincts are the result of gradual development, there must have been a time when the bee knew nothing of honey gathering, wax manufacturing, cell construction, or royal jelly preparation. If that be true, the whole family must inevitably have perished. The first bees knew as much as their modern mates, and so, must have been born with qualities conferred by their Creator.

Evolution depends on heredity for the accumulation of characters. That is, parents must hand on to their children powers which they have acquired, the children in turn, passing down the improvements they have succeeded in developing. Apart from the acknowledged fact that acquired characteristics are not trans-

—17—

mitted, in the case of the bee, the father or drone bee has nothing to transmit. He can not make honey or wax, has no pollen basket and is an almost useless encumbrance. The queen bee, too, is totally destitute of the powers which characterize the workers, just as the drone, so neither of the parents possess anything to hand down to their progeny. Then where could the worker bee get its powers, unless in the first moment of its existence from the Supreme Architect?

The animal world is full of just such examples as these, and to the unbiased mind would seem to offer incontrovertible evidence of an Omnipotent guiding Hand.

The human body, also, abounds in proofs of design. It is possible to mention but a very few of these wonders, so amazing in themselves, that they preclude the possibility of chance development. If literally, scores of structures in our bodies bear in themselves the unmistakable imprint of a Designer, who will logically deny the existence of a personal God?

When any portion of the human body is examined under the microscope it is found to be made up of many small parts called cells. These are the living bricks which compose the house in which we live.

Every blade of grass, every weed, every flower, every tree, every animal, whether it live in the water, on the land, or in the air, is composed of cells. Dead materials, on the other hand, are not made of cells, but only living things. Each cell is a bit of transparent, jelly-like material, called protoplasm. It is like the albumen of an egg, but, of its amazing powers, we know very little. The life principle which was breathed into this substance in the beginning, eludes all our investigations.

—18—

Each cell in the body has the same needs as the little one-celled animal which lives alone. But each body cell cannot take care of itself like the tiny animals which they so much resemble. The body cells in their various activities are marked by a division of labor, and yet all unite and work for the good of the whole community. Like the animals, each cell must have food, must have oxygen, and must get rid of its poisonous wastes. By their marvelous systems of coordination, it is possible for them to live and reproduce themselves while serving faithfully the body to which they belong.

The cells are divided into groups of specialists. The cells of the stomach digest the food; the bone cells build up a strong frame-work to support the body; the muscle cells move the body; the kidney cells throw out wastes; the lung cells take in oxygen from the air; and the red blood cells of the blood carry oxygen through all the body to the cells. Each cell, then, is a skilled workman doing some particuar work for the body as a whole, not an unskilled laborer trying to do all the many different kinds of work necessary to provide for its own wants.

It can be clearly understood that in order to have a properly functioning body, there must be efficiently working cells, and a fine degree of cooperation among all. If any group of cells fails in its work, all the cells must suffer, and death to the body would result.

The resemblance between the body and a community of people is striking. In any community, we have individuals of different occupations,—doctors, teachers, carpenters, blacksmiths, grocers, and milkmen. In the body, there are muscle cells, bone cells, digestive cells, and many others. In both systems there is mutual interdependence.

The carpenter builds houses for the milkman and the grocer, and these persons bring the carpenter his food. So, the stomach cells digest food for the cells of the lungs, and the lung cells take in oxygen for the stomach cells.

Tissues and organs are made up of groups of cells, in each tissue the individuals doing their own particular work. An organ is a part of the body doing a special work. In the beautiful organization and specialization of these microscopic bits of living protoplasm, and in their marvellous coordination all for the welfare of the individual, we see clearly a definite plan.

Every system in the body is full of wonders. The nervous system has for its first great work, the harmonious working of all parts of the body. Its second work is to act as the organ of the mind. Nerves are elongated threads made up of many cells connected together. Most of these nerve fibres originate in the brain, and are designed to carry messages to and from that organ. Thus messages are carried from the brain to the muscles causing them to contract, and to all glands and organs of the body, putting them all to work at their proper time. Other nerves carry communications from the different parts of the body to the brain and spinal cord, in order to keep these parts informed as to those conditions which so quickly and profoundly affect them.

Marked evidence of design in the construction of the body, is seen in the fact that all the different parts of the body are brought into intimate connection through the agency of the brain and spinal cord acting as central office. The central nervous system consists of the brain, the spinal cord and the nerves arising from the brain and cord. Twelve pairs of nerves pass out from the brain, and thirty-one pairs from the cord, putting the great nerve centers in touch with all parts of the body. The spinal cord weighs about an ounce, the brain about 50 ounces.

A layer of nerve cells on the surface of the brain, called the gray matter, has the mind in association with it. The cerebrum comprises three quarters of the brain, and is the seat of the mind, the seat of the sensations, and it originates and sends out impulses that cause voluntary movements.

The mind is the king which sits upon the throne of reason and directs the operations of the body. When the 1,200,000,000 cells which compose the outer layer of precious gray matter, are injured or destroyed, memory, reason and intelligence are lost.

Nerve messages from all parts of the body come into the cerebrum and cause the sensations of light, sound, taste, smell, touch, heat, cold, hunger, fatigue, and other sensations.

When we decide to move, the cerebrum or the mind situated somewhere in the cerebrum, is able to start impulses which cause the muscles to contract or shorten, and therefore we have the power, in health, of voluntary movement.

The little brain or cerebellum, lying behind and below the cerebrum, enables all the muscles to maintain a proper amount of contraction, and also assists in co-ordinating the muscles of locomotion. When the cerebellum is, from any cause, not able to do its proper work, the body finds it difficult to maintain the erect position, and the individual staggers about as though intoxicated. This orderly supervision of the movements involved in standing, walking and running, which the little brain exercises, appear to indicate forethought in the One who originated it.

Another important nerve center is called the medulla, lying at the back and lower portion of the brain and the upper part of the spinal cord. It really connects the higher parts of the brain with the spinal cord and the body. The greater part of the head and many of the internal organs, including the heart and lungs, are supplied by nerves that arise from the medulla. Injury to the medulla causes death by interference with breathing.

The spinal cord which is enclosed in a bony canal formed by an ingenious arrangement of the separate bones which comprise the spine, has the same functions as the medulla, conducting impulses to and from the brain, and acting also as a reflex center. Reflex actions are caused by impulses which start in nerves leading from the surface of the body to the brain. Its meaning may be illustrated in this way. If a finger is burned by touching a flame, the heat starts an impulse along the nerve fibres. This impulse passes into the spinal cord, then into the nerve leading from the cord out to the muscles. This last impulse causes the muscles to contract and the hand is jerked away, quite involuntarily.

An impulse also goes up to the brain and causes a sensation of pain, but the hand is moved before the pain is felt. Any action like this is a reflex action. This action which is necessary to quick response on the part of the muscles, and is planned to save the individual from injury, certainly points to a designing Intelligence. It works automatically and without the conscious cooperation of the rest of the body.

A flea bites an elephant's tail. The elephant is annoyed and decides to lash its tail in order to shake off the flea. What was it that travelled so quickly up along the nerve wire to the elephant's spinal cord and brain, giving the sensation of irritation resulting in the muscular contraction of the offended tail, a contraction which caused it to move with sufficient rapidity to dislodge the tiny tormentor? Was this impulse a group of electrons, a charge of negative electricity? How account for this mechanism which operates so instantaneously and so uniformly for the comfort of the individual's body? Will chance, evolutionary development satisfy our inquiry?

We lie asleep in a room with the blinds up and the sun shining outside. A ray of light filters through the window and strikes us on the forehead, but we sleep on. Presently it impinges on our eyelid, and on through the pupil to the sensitive fibres of the optic nerve. The muscles of the eyelid suddenly begin to function, we open our eyes and are awake. What caused this phenomenon? Why did we not waken when the light fell on the skin? Why are the cells of the optic nerve more sensitive to light than those of the skin? The sunlight radiates heat as well as light. Why did not out skin detect the heat and waken us? What is heat and what is light?

Ether wave vibrations of a frequency of 3,000 billion to 800,000 billion per second cause us to experience the sensation of radiant heat, when these vibrations strike the skin. Vibrations to the numbers of 400,000 billion to 800,000 billion per second falling on our retina cause us to experience what is called light and color. The vibrations are the same kind but of differing frequency. The nerves or conducting wires of the skin are not so sensitive as the nerves of the eye. Certain electric waves below 3,000 billion vibrations

—23—

per second are not sensed, nor are ultra-violet and x-rays, which are caused by the inconceivably rapid vibrations in ether, amounting to 800,000 billion to 6,000,000,000 billion per second.

Similar conditions abound in our bodies. The skin, for instance, is crowded with little sense organs, consisting of sensitive bulbs underneath the skin, the terminations of these nerves or telegraph wires running from the great nerve centers. Most of the sense organs are for announcing "pain." That is, when danger threatens, a bell is rung in the brain, which, obeying the signal, sends along another wire, a command intended to prevent the danger from harming unduly the victim.

Other little bulbs, like those on the end of our fingers, provide us with the delicate sense of touch. Others feel cold, while still another set registers heat. Other little bulbs standing up like a regiment of soldiers on the upper surface of the tongue are taste-buds. The tip of the tongue especially appreciates sweet substances while the back part recognizes bitterness.

Nerves from a certain centre in the brain end in a cavity of the nose, and act as sentinels against dangers which announce themselves in the air and are detected as odors. A very strong offensive substance like mercaptan can be sensed even if there is but one part in 25,000,000,000,000 times as much air, so extremely sensitive is this apparatus. And yet, we are told that the sense of smell is degenerating!

But what shall be said of the special organ for sight, —the eye? The essential part of the mechanism of this sense is the eyeball and the nerve which goes from this to the sight-centre in the brain. The eye is the most remarkable camera in the world.

— 24 —

We have a roundish ball made of dense and very strong fibrous tissue. The one-sixth part which bulges out in front and which is known as the cornea, is transparent, while the remaining five-sixths is opaque.

Behind the cornea and separated from it by a watery fluid, is a wonderful curtain with an opening in the middle of it, which works automatically to adapt the eye to the intensity or the light which falls on it. Fibres of muscles are so ingeniously distributed in it that it is able almost to close the opening in a strong light, or open it wide when the light is fainter.

Behind the circular window or pupil, is another unique feature, the crystalline lens which surpasses any other lens of which we know. Fine and delicately acting muscles automatically alter its shape so that it can be focused for any distance.

The eyeball is set in a wonderful socket of seven bones, protected in this safe place by an overhanging ridge of bone, and by a line of hair, the eyebrows, which prevent perspiration from falling on the eyeball. There is a remarkable watering system to keep the sensitive eyeball continually washed free of dust and a canal to carry off excess fluid. There is also an oiling system and the ball is moved in different directions by a set of six muscles, one of which is slung over a pulley! Can these be chance arrangements?

But the most wonderful of all is the "sensitive plate" at the back of the eye-ball. Here are spread out 338,000 nerve fibres running to the brain; 3,360,000 retinal cones in which some mysterious chemical action seems to take place. But in none of these parts is vision accomplished. When the light from an object is reflected back through the window, the pupil, through the lens, and strikes the spread-out optic nerve fibres, then, there is telegraphed a message to the sight center in the brain, which interprets for us what we are looking at. So, that, the place where we actually see, is a spot where absolute darkness reigns.

The organ of hearing is scarcely less remarkable. A narrow channel, about an inch long, runs from the external ear to the drum. This canal is protected by a bitter tasting wax, which very effectively keeps off adventurous insects. Sound waves pass along this short channel, and beat upon the sensitive drum, the tympanum, a membrane of most ingenious construction. It has no period of vibration of its own but responds immediately and accurately to every sort of wave which strikes it. Therefore, it is so made that every part has a different period of vibration, and it is "damped" by a little bone which presses on it from the other side.

The pressure of air on the inside of this drum must be the same as on the outside, so this is regulated by a channel running to the inner side of it from the roof of the mouth.

Three little bones, the hammer, anvil and stirrup, convey the vibrations from the outer drum to another drum stretched across the entrance to the real ear inside of the skull. Beyond this again is a coiled shell which contains the real organ of hearing, a large number of hair cells—"organs of Corti"—interlacing with the fine fibres of the nerve or hearing, which convey the movement straight to the brain center. Could mechanisms like these possibly make themselves?

A fascinating study are the ductless guands, the most remarkable chemists in the body. They extract substances from the blood and then secrete certain

—26—

"chemical messengers" which carry instructions to various parts of the body, giving definite orders which are always carried out.

Sir Arthur Keith, in his book, "The Human Body," writes concerning the substance or hormone, which is secreted in order to stimulate the glands of digestion: "The secretin or hormone, which acts as a missive, is posted in the nearest letter-boxes or capillaries (smallest bood-vessels) in the duodenal wall (wall of the first part of the small bowel at the junction with the stomach) and is carried away in the general blood circulation, which serves for all kinds of postal traffic. In a postal system where there are no sorters and which must be conducted by an automatic mechanism, letters or missives cannot be addressed in the usual way. Their destination is indicated, not by their inscription, but by their shape. The molecules of secretin may be regarded as ultra-microscopic Yale keys sent out to search for the locks of letter-boxes which they can fit and enter. They circulate around the body until they find their destination. What is still more wonderful in this system is that the letter-boxes, or we may call them locks, have a positive attraction for the key missives which are intended for them."

The chemical stuff, or hormone, secreted by the thyroid glands in the neck increases the vitality of the tissues by making them more greedy for oxygen, so that the work goes on more briskly.

Then there is the thymus gland situated in front of the breast bone, which acts to prevent the organs peculiar to the male and female, from developing too early.

Up in the head is a little and long-neglected tissue, called the "pituitary body" which controls the growth of the body. Dwarfs have an undeveloped pituitary gland while giants have too much of it.

The body is supplied with mechanisms for every emergency. It is able to adjust itself to changes in the temperature. If there is too much heat, the millions of sweat glands in the skin immedately begin to act to throw off the heat-laden fluid and thus reduce the temperature to safe and comfortable limits. The little nerves which control the size of the blood vessels in the skin and so the amount of the blood flowing through it, get in their work and the vessels are dilated. The blood floods the skin and the heat evaporates rapidly.

The operations of the human system, and indeed those also of the lower animal kingdom, which are necessary to life, are carried on quite automatically. Thus, when we lie down to sleep, the "great restorer" comes without wooing, nor do we have to plan how to keep our respiration going during the unconscious hours of the night. Our heart beats regularly 72 times to the minute, four times as fast as the respiratory act, and we need pay no attention to it. In itself it contains a marvellous mechanism which looks after the proper functioning of the mighty pump which forces the life-fluid so ceaselessly throughout the entire system.

The process of digestion presents many unexplainable wonders to the inquiring mind. We take in a great variety of food several times a day, and often speak of the mouth watering at the sight or smell of it. This is an interesting reflex action. The olfactory nerves of smell in the nose, detecting the odor which foretells the imminent approach of that which is so much desired, telegraphs the message to the brain,— "Food is coming, get ready." In response to this information, a command is issued to the salivary glands in the mouth,—important organs of digestion—to secrete immediately the juices which help to prepare the food for assimilation into the system. So instant is the response, that the mouth fills with saliva even before we see the food. Here again, we have an automatic system which the materialist will have trouble in explaining.

The microscopic cells in the salivary glands which make the saliva, are such remarkable chemical machines that no one can understand them. Although the saliva is 99 per cent water, it yet contains chemicals which begin the digestion of starchy food, converting it to a kind of sugar. In addition, they, of course, make a soft pulp of the food and so assist in the swallowing act.

When teeth and salivary glands have done their work, and the little taste buds on the back of the tongue have had their brief moment of satisfaction, the mouthful of pulp is swallowed. Keith describes the act in this way: "Swallowing seems such an easy and automatic act that we are quite unaware of the elaborate system of signals, side-shunts, and level-crossings which have to be manipulated to permit the busy traffic of the pharynx to pass unchecked."

J. Arthur Thomson puts the wonder picturesquely. He says: "The whole mouth changes. Certain sensitive spots at the back of the mouth—electric press-buttons, we may call them—give the signal that the food is ready. The muscles which closed the back of the mouth while we are masticating, relax. The lower jaw is pressed against the upper. The soft palate forms an inclined plane. Other muscles close the airways to the nose and the great airways to the lungs. The whole

—29—

complex machine acts together and pumps the food into the first part of the alimentary tube, the pharynx."

And then ensue a number of things which can only be understood when we postulate a Designer who worked out the abstruse problems of the body with unerring skill.

When the food is emptied into the stomach, it begins a long and interesting journey. It has a twenty-eight foot tube to travel through, and in which it must be broken up physically and chemically before it is ready to be utilized by the system.

As one sits at the table, the sight and smell of roast beef telegraph their news to a certain nerve-center in the brain, from which a silent message of stimulation goes to the myriads of glands lining the inner wall of the stomach. The messages are multiplied when the taste buds on the tongue are tickled by agreeable sensations. The blood gathers on the wall of the stomach, and the little glands immediately utilize this fluid to manufacture the digestive juice which is poured out on the food.

But digestion is only begun in the stomach, and only a little of the food is absorbed there. The nitrogenous or protein food like flesh, fish and eggs, is broken up still further and prepared for absorption, while the sugars, starches and fats, are passed on to the next department, into the twenty-foot laboratory, the narrow, "small intestine."

The glandular chemists take the alkaline blood, and from this manufacture an acid fluid by a process which no one understands. When the acidulated food from the stomach, at the end of an hour or two, is permitted to make its exit through the valvular opening into the first portion of the small intestine, the touch of it on the walls of this latter tube, causes the intestinal glands to secrete a marvellous chemical, called secretin, and pour it into the blood. Hurrying on its way, carried by the blood stream, secretin goes straight to its destination, which is another important organ of digestion, the pancreas. Although the hormone, secretin, goes through the entire body, it acts solely on the pancres. When the chemical message is duly received and its purport understood, the pancreas at once sets to work more vigorously and empties an increased supply of digestive juice into the small intestine.

The pancreatic juice is able to dissolve and make into an emulsion, the starches, sugars, and fats, as well as the nitrogenous foods. The thick creamy fluid,— the pulped and semi-digested food, moves slowly along the bowel, at the rate of about one inch a second. The interior wall of this tube is lined not only with glands but with tiny fingers which stand out, microscopically, "like the pile on fine velvet." These fingers reach out and take in the passing food, which, by an ingenious arrangement of channels, is presently all gathered up into one duct lying on the left side of the spinal column, and carried up to the root of the neck where it is emptied into the blood stream. Once here is passes through the liver, and is then pumped round the body so that the various organs and tissues may easily select from it the nourishment they need.

The body seems to have a very efficient cafeteria system, in which the food may be imagined as loaded on a train of flat cars, each kind laid out in orderly piles so as to be easily accessible to the hungry cells. The train passes slowly but uniformly along. One set of cells are on the lookout for some sugar. They wait patiently until the load comes to them, then reach out their tiny fingers, quickly take a glance at the different assortments, fill their hands with what they require, and retire as the train-load goes on out of sight. In a short time they will require more food, perhaps starches or fats, and if their owner is functioning properly, they will find the cafeteria train coming along on time to supply their ever-recurring needs.

May we ask, how food-trains like these can be prepared and dispatched with such amazing ease and regularity, and how each individual cell in the body knows how to satisfy its wants, unless behind the work there be a Master-Workman, a central Controller or Manager who sees that the machinery is properly and accurately constructed, and kept in efficient working order?

A few hundred years ago, the blood was thought to be a very simple fluid, and not much attention was paid to it, in spite of the fact that if man lost enough of it, he invariably died. In 1629 Sir William Harvey discovered the circulation of the blood in the body. Before that date, air was thought to pass through the vessels, and the word, "artery" is derived from the Latin word, aer, meaning air. So it is only recently that we have discovered the supreme importance of the blood, but, strange to say, thousands of years ago, Moses had this information given to him, when he declared in Leviticus, "The life of the flesh is in the blood." How did this old writer, reared in the Egyptian court where as far as we know, nothing of this was known, come to make this epoch-making pronouncement, destined to be overlooked by a skeptical science which looks on the Bible as out of date and especially antiquated in its science? Will logic and

—32—

common-sense permit of any other solution than that the scribe got his knowledge from one Omniscient Creator?

Even a superficial knowledge of the composition and capabilities of the blood, must prove that it has been designed to carry out just those functions which it performs with such apparent ease.

In the blood, there are myriads of small round red particles or cells called corpuscles. These little discs derive their color from a peculiar chemical by the name of haemoglobin which has a great affinity for oxygen and carries it from the lungs to the tissues. In every cubic millimetre there are about five million of these cells. In the entire body there are about twenty-five thousand trillions of them. They are formed, chiefly, in the red marrow of bones, and, after serving for a few weeks, are broken up in the liver or spleen.

Besides these red cells, or oxygen-carriers, there are in the blood a great army of defenders against germs. When bacteria gain entrance to the body, these brave fighters rush from all parts, and a battle royal ensues. These cells which are colorless, and are known as white corpuscles or leucocytes, have a summary method of dealing with intruders. They surround their enemies and engulf them. If they prove strong enough to devour the microbes, we are saved from infection, if not, illness follows.

The wonderful mechanisms of the body are never-ending source of fascination to the student. When bacteria enter, they immediately begin to produce a poison or toxin, which causes the symptoms from which the patient suffers. The blood acts just as promptly and commences to form an opposing substance

—33—

to conteract the harmful effect of the bacterial posion. This is called anti-toxin, and is a chemical, which will, if given time and proper conditions, perfectly neutralize the toxin. The blood has the amazing power to manufacture a defensive anti-toxin for every conceivable germ infection.

Sir Arthur Keith, in "The Engines of the Human Body," refers to "the immense and movable armies of microscopic corpuscles which can be mobilized for police or sanitary duties. They swarm in the blood as it circulates round the body. .. . it is extremely probable that one variety of them, if not more, are really errand-boys on their way to deliver parcels or messages, and that the gland masses which are built up in and around lymph channels, serve both as nurseries for the upbringing of such messengers, and also as offices from which they are dispatched on their errands."

Without subjecting the imagination to any undue strain, it would appear that these things undoubtedly prove a definite plan to save the body from injurious infections and resulting death. If it were not for these provisions, every body would, long since, have suffered death. The enemies of the body have always existed, and if these powers were non-existent in the first instance and had to be evolved, there would have been no hope for the first animals or men, deprived of their necessary means of defense. That means that the earliest ancestors had these mechanisms in perfect working order, and must have received them as a gift from the One who brought the body into being.

The Bible makes no particular effort to prove the existence of God. That is taken for granted. The Bible never argues, it announces. It does not strive to explain the great truths on which the Christian faith is built. It simply proclaims them.

The Bible does, however, issue a bold and dauntless challenge to a skeptical science to prove it guilty of fraud, fallacy or fabrication. We read in the twelfth chapter of Job at the 7th verse: "But ask now the beasts, and they shall teach thee; and the fowls of the air and they shall tell thee: or speak to the earth and it shall teach thee: and the fishes of the sea shall declare unto thee. Who knoweth not in all these that the hand of the Lord hath done this?"

The Bible professes to be a divine Revelation from a personal God. It is the Record of God's dealings with sinful men, their Fall, and the Remedy He has provided for their ultimate restoration and salvation. It is permeated with the idea of the existence of God, in fact, that is the foundation on which it is constructed.

The Bible has never been proved to be in error in a single instance. It has proved itself a thousand times the inerrant Revelation from God Himself. A Book written with such sustained dignity and mellifluous precision, abounding in lightning-like phrases, arrows shot from the quiver of Infallible Wisdom, exhibiting the supernatural prescience of prophecy, contemptuously indifferent to the flippant insolence of a decadent skepticism, miraculously anticipating by thirty centuries the most stupendous discoveries of modern times, is not a patchwork of grotesque stupidity, incorporating a thousand mangled delusions, a monstrous travesty of Truth,—but is the flawless and exalted embodiment of Omniscience, the supreme Gift from the omnipotent Ruler and Creator of the universe.

As the result of our study, two great truths must never be forgotten,—the Eternal Father still lives; and only "the fool hath said in his heart, 'there is no God.'"

Men, Monkeys and Missing Links

By
ARTHUR I. BROWN
M.D., C.M., F.R.C.S.E.
Vancouver, B. C.

PRICE TWENTY-FIVE CENTS

May 1st, 1923

1006 Nelson St.
Vancouver, B. C.

ARTHUR I. BROWN
M.D., C.M., F.R.C.S.E.

Men, Monkeys and Missing Links

The title of this booklet is not intended to convey the impression that evolutionists claim direct relationship for the human race with the monkey. We are informed that our ancestor was some "unknown" and vanished anthropoid. Monkeys, according to the latest pronouncement of science, occupy only one branch of this common family tree.

Professor Henry Fairfield Osborn of the American Museum of Natural History, New York, says on page 4 of Guide Leaflet Series No. 52, May, 1921: "Man is not descended from any known form of ape, either living or fossil." But he still believes that he is descended from something of which there is not the slightest trace. And this is called "Science"!

The writer will deal only with the "missing link" phase of evolution, and the subject will be discussed wholly from a scientific standpoint. Much of the argument and most of the facts are taken from Alfred Watterson McCann's book, "God—or Gorilla," the most scathing and unanswerable indictment ever published against this untenable hypothesis. For those interested in the question, but without the opportunity or inclination to read this great work, a synopsis of a small portion of it, with the addition of other relevant data, will be helpful.

The assertions of the evolutionists are strikingly dogmatic, and the conclusions drawn from certain discoveries are said to prove beyond a doubt that man has developed from some lower form of life.

An example of the absurdly grotesque extremes to which some scientific writers are prepared to go, is to be found in a series of articles on "The Story of Man and His World" now appearing in "Popular Science" under the signature of Professor E. E. Free, Ph. D., Fellow of the American Association for the Advancement of Science. The article in the May number, 1923, has an additional sponsor, Professor Wm. K. Gregory, Curator of Comparative Anatomy, American Museum of Natural History. The article is titled: "Man—An Invention," and attempts to show how our first ancestor, a "speck of sea-slime," decided that it would like to possess the power of motion, and so proceeded to invent muscle! Then followed a wonderful series of "inventions"—bone, blood, warm blood, legs, backbone, organs, etc. Strange to say, very late in the process, when considerable of this amazing and difficult work had been accomplished after millions of years of hard labor and planning, a "brain capable of real thinking" was produced! One may be pardoned for expressing the conviction that a brain and some "real thinking" were necessary for the "invention" of muscle, bone, blood, etc! The article is a scientific monstrosity, but is constantly being duplicated by presumably educated scientific authors, considered to be authorities. How can any sane individual swallow such clap-trap? Impossible!

We are told also that man has been in existence on this planet for a period of some 500,000 years. The scientific world was shocked when Theodore Moreaux, Director of the Observatory at Bourges, entered the controversy in February, 1921, and asserted that these extraordinary figures, as all the fossils show, are preposterous and that the human race cannot boast of more than a few thousands of years instead of the hundreds of thousands claimed by certain palaentologists.

The length of time since the glacial period is important as showing how long man has been on the earth. It is interesting to note that the ice-age experts unanimously repudiate the half-million year period. Planck names 20,000 years, De Geers 9,000, Sollas 7,000, while Wright, the foremost American authority, furnishes much evidence to prove that 5,000 years covers all the requirements of science.

These calculations, which cannot be laughed out of court, make the estimates of the evolutionists look ridiculous, but they are apparently ignored by the men determined to prove an ape ancestry for the human race.

Professor Arthur Keith, an eminent evolutionist authority, with no evidence whatever, demands 350,000 years for the period which has elapsed since the glacial skeletons were buried. Keith is an anthropologist of the highest standing, but does not profess to rank as a geologist. George Frederick Wright is an eminent geologist who makes no profession of expertness in anatomy. Wright says—"The Origin and Antiquity of Man," 1912, page 195: "Large areas in Europe and North America which are now principal centers of civilization were buried under glacial ice thousands of feet thick, while the civilization of Babylonia (5,000 to 6,000 years ago) was in its heyday. The glib manner in which many, not to say most, popular writers speak of the Glacial Epoch as far distant in geological time, is due to ignorance of facts which would seem to be so clear that he who runs might read."

The same confusion exists in regard to the many guesses at the age of the world. Astronomers, basing their estimates on energy and heat, conclude that this planet came into existence 100,000,000 years ago. Geologists, on the other hand, are quite certain the world is at least 500,000,000 years old—a slight discrepancy of 400,000,000 years! The truth is that the conclusions of science are often the merest guesswork and have changed times without number.

If evolution is accepted as a fact, that is, if the human body has been evolved from simple forms of plant and animal life, the simple becoming complex by gradual changes in form and feature, and in size, shape and function of the various organs, these changes extending over millions of years, then, necessarily there must have been intermediary forms or links between species. It cannot be too strongly emphasized that these connecting links are absolutely essential, must have existed and ought to be found somewhere in the world if we are to believe the theory. New and higher species must have come from earlier and lower species, this process being repeated over and over again until ultimately, after aeons of time, man was produced.

Professor Vernon Kellogg, of Leland Stanford University, in his "Darwinism To-day," 1908, page 18, says: "Speaking by and large we only tell the general truth when we declare that no indubitable cases of species-forming or transforming, that is, of descent, have been observed." And then on page 29 we find these words: "For my part it seems better to go back to the old and safe 'Ignoramus' standpoint." If the evolutionists themselves admit the absence of all evidence of changing species, what becomes of their theory that connecting links between species have existed?

And yet the four corners of the earth have been and are being searched for fossil remains, the bony remnants of these elusive curiosities. Many expeditions have hopefully wended their way into the heart of the Old World, only to return unsuccessful.

Raymond L. Ditmars, curator of mammals and reptiles of the Zoological Gardens, Bronx Park, New York City, is a firm believer in the theory that "our apish grandsires chattered love amid the cocoanut branches of the unexplored jungles long before Adam ever lost his spare-rib or Paris rolled the little red apple." In the New York Evening Telegram of August 28, 1921, he writes: "When the evasive missing link is eventually found he will be discovered tightly grasping the paw of his mate and chattering such monkey gibberish in her ears as 'Don't be afraid. We're their ancestors, you know.'"

The same article announces that Ditmars is making a picture, 20,000 feet of reel, to convince the rankest unbeliever that the anthropoid apes are our real ancestors, and that these pictures are being made while an expedition, headed by Roy Andrews, is pushing into Tibet with 75 camels, four motor trucks, and four Handley-Page airplanes in search of the missing link, which Dr. Andrews expects to find in the form of an anthropoid ape a thousand years advanced in evolution over the type of ape we see in captivity.

According to Ditmars, "This is the highbrow ape; it stands erect, supposedly, and displays all the characteristics of man. He will be brought back, with sufficient of his brothers and sisters, to permit a searching investigation as to his relation to humans. Only patience is needed." More than 60 years ago Sir Charles Lyell wrote in "Antiquity of Man," page 499: "At present we must be content to wait patiently, and not to allow our judgment to be influenced by want of evidence, * * * in equatorial Africa, and in certain islands of the East Inidan Archipelago, may we hope to meet hereafter with lost types of primates allied to the gorilla, chimpanzee and ourang-outang."

Sixty years have passed, and we still wait. "How long, O Lord, how long?"

In 1898, Haeckel published "The Last Link," and uses the phrase "an historical fact" in referring to the existence of this missing link. In 1906, another work by the same author, "Last Words on Evolution," gave his own pedigree of the primates, a wholly imaginary product, consisting of a mixture of absolutely fictitious creatures with really existing creatures, the connection between them being as fictitious as the fictions themselves.

And yet the editor of a prominent New York daily as late as June, 1921, uses the following words in giving expression to his unswerving faith: "None but a fool would dare criticize the theory of man's descent from an ape, because it is the commonly accepted opinion of mankind." Whom shall we follow—this cock-sure amateur or an eminent scientist like Professor W Branco of the Geological and Palaentological Institute of Berlin University, who, in his closing address at the Fifth International Congress of Zoologists held in Berlin, August 16th, 1901, took as his subject, "Fossil Man," and completely refuted Haeckel's "historical fact," "The Last Link"?

The principal facts brought out by Branco are these: It is possible to trace the ancestry of most of our present mammals among the fossils of the Tertiary period. Man appears suddenly in the Quaternary period. There is no record of any ancestor of man in the Tertiary period. The very first evidence of man's existence on this planet, and all other evidence thus far established, proves that he made his first appearance at once as a complete true man.

Erick Wasmann, in "Modern Biology," page 478, and H. Obermaier, in "L'Anthropologie," confirm Branco when he comes to the truly scientific conclusion: "Palaentology tells us nothing on the subject—it knows no ancestors of man."

Professor Johannes Ranke, at the Anthropological Congress, Lindau, in 1899, speaking of this hypothetical common ancestor of men and apes, said: "Whilst a charming picture of the past and possibly of the future is being shown us, and whilst a fanciful design is being carried out in all directions, we are, as a rule, in quest of facts, not theories. * * * I must protest against the assumption that these facts have been really furnished by zoology and palaentology any more than by anatomy. All else is still a matter of hypothesis—a work merely of the imagination."

Erick Wasmann, in his book, "Modern Biology and the Theory of Evolution," page 463, adds to this as follows: "We have the pedigree of the present apes, a pedigree very rich in species and coming down from the hypothetical ancestor form of the oldest Tertiary period to the present day. Zittel's 'Grandzuge der Palaontologie' gives a list of no fewer than 30 genera of fossil Pro-Simiae and 18 genera of fossil apes, the remains of which are buried in the various strata from the Lower Eocene to the close of the Alluvial epoch, but not one connecting link has been found between

MEN, MONKEYS AND MISSING LINKS

their hypothetical ancestral forms and man at the present time. The whole hypothetical pedigree of man is not supported by a single fossil genus or a single fossil species."

How extraordinary! If man were really descended from a pre-historic ancestor common to him and the apes at the present day, there must surely be some fossil trace left of his existence and not merely traces of apes. Why does palaeontology furnish so many and such wonderful specimens of fossil apes and not a single specimen of a hypothetical ancestor of man if they really lived side by side, as is the claim?

Prof. Osborn, ever ready with an attempt to explain the unexplainable, offers the following delicious morsel for our consideration: "Although the ancestors of man lived partly among trees and forests, they lived chiefly on the ground, where they were entombed by floods and sand-storms." Now we understand the very mysterious disappearance of Grandfather and Grandmother Ape-like Ancestor!

The same scientists have found no difficulty in discovering the fossil remains of hundreds of the ancestors of the horse and other animals who lived "chiefly" on the ground, as well as those of monkeys and great apes of every description.

Then will someone please explain why, if the floods and sand-storms entombed all the remains of ape-men and sub-men, the same floods and sand-storms spared the fossil remains of the countless scores of smaller animals now on exhibition in all the museums of the world?

During the past 50 years several small pieces of bone have been discovered by the indefatigable fossil-hunters, and from these insignificant portions remarkable and imaginary "reconstructions" have been made, which we are asked to believe are authentic and reliable representations of individuals once living as members of distinct races. These are labelled and exhibited as "missing links," and to look at them one might suppose, as many do, that they are photographs or faithful and true reproductions in form and feature of our ape-men predecessors. The fact is not stressed that they are purely hypothetical curiosities constructed from a few bits of bone that one might hold in the palm of the hand. Certainly not! A "missing link" is necessary for our evolutionist friends, and if such a thing cannot be found, the only way out is to manufacture an imaginery one, hoping that those who gaze and read wide-eyed and open-mouthed, will not have the temerity to inquire too closely into the method of bringing these weird and wholly unscientific monstrosities on the stage for our inspection.

But we are really most curious and our inquisitiveness will not be denied. Prof. Osborn, before whom American evolutionists bow as their leading authority, in his exhibit now in the Hall of the Age of Man, American Museum of Natural History, New York City, shows four cases containing what he terms half-ape, half-human remains in an attempt to prove our ape ancestry.

Let us look at these four antiques and then take a brief glance at most of the other skeletons or portions of skeletons discovered at different times in various parts of the world, and used to bolster up a very wobbly hypothesis. We shall find that the supports have completely given way and the superstructure reared upon them by scientists is a hopeless mass of ruins.

The four wonderful "half and halfs" are "The Trinil Ape-Man or Pithecanthropus Erectus" (ape-man standing upright), "The Heidleberg Man," "The Gibraltar and Neanderthal Man," and "The Piltdown Man." Rather a close examination will also be made of "The Rhodesian Man," and a few observations on other skeletons and bones of lesser importance.

In discussing all these imaginary ape-men, much is made of brain-pan capacities expressed in cubic centimeters. The largest ape skull has a capacity of about 600 c.c., while the average cranial capacity of the males of Central Europe to-day is about 1503 c.c. Prof. Osborn accepts the doctrine of the materialistic school which declares that the capacity of the skull affords a direct indication of the mental capabilities of its owner. Thus, a half-ape, half-man should show a skull of somewhere near 1000 or 1100 c.c. We shall see how this capacity is conveniently arranged. One is reminded of the old saying, "Figures never lie, but liars often figure."

Apparently the scientists do not know of the Weddas, a certainly human race of dwarfs from Ceylon, who have a skull capacity of 960 c. c., which is very much smaller but ought to be very much larger than the skull capacity of a creature described as "500,000 years old."

It is unfortunate for the purposes of the evolutionists that few human beings today have a cranial capacity greater than that of the sub-human beings whose "restorations" inhabit the "Hall of the Age of Man"—better termed the "Hall of Confusion." It was once thought that the enormous 1965 c. c. skull of Bismarck was about the biggest thing of its kind in the world. But Professor Rudolf Virchow discovered a larger one measuring 2010 c. c., and strange to relate, it belonged not to a poet or statesman of Great Britain, Germany or France; not to any creature of any civilized nation, but to a savage of Great Britain!

One of the stumbling blocks created by Professor Osborn himself, but nowhere referred to by himself, is found in the fact that the old paleolithic skulls described as Neanderthal, and said to be 50,000 years old, had an average capacity of 1625-1635 c. c. Some of them even measure up to 1700 c. c. And so the bottom is knocked out of the argument, which nevertheless continues to be used. Again we ask, is this Science?

(1) THE TRINIL APE-MAN, OR PITHECANTHROPUS ERECTUS

Professor Osborn and others speak of the discovery of the Trinil "Race" in Central Java, thousands of pre-humans living 500,000 years ago. The guide leaflet which is given the visitor to the Hall of the Age of Man, Museum of Natural History, New York City, draws attention to "five cases in the center of the Hall, devoted to the story of man," which he states contain "reproductions of ALL of the notable specimens that have been discovered." The whole original lot will perhaps fill a peach-basket!

The leaflet tells us of "the progressive increase of relative intelligence appreciated by the most casual observer," and draws our notice to certain "anatomical characters" such as "the increased prominence of the chin, the reduction of the eyebrow ridges, the reduction of the prominence of the lower face as a whole, the increased size of skull and brain capacity."

Osborn holds that the African negro and the Asiatic Chinaman have not evolved as far as the modern European whites. If this is true, we should expect to find the above-mentioned anatomical characteristics more pronounced in the negroes and Chinese. But Professor Arthur Keith, frequently quoted by Osborn, at this point throws the monkey wrench into the machinery. In his book, "The Human Body," 1910, page 177, he says: "In the typical African negro the forehead as a rule is high and the supraorbital ridges are distinctly less prominent than in the European. The supraorbital (above the eye) ridges of the Chinaman are less developed than in the European."

The "Restored Head" of the Trinil Ape-Man is made from a tiny bit of bone weighing a few ounces, and is designed to show a half-human, half-ape resemblance. This use of it is inexplicable in view of Prof. Osborn's assertion that "The Trinil Ape-Man is the first of the conundrums in human history." Then he asks a pertinent question which he does not answer: "IS the Trinil Race (?) pre-human or not?"

The popular opinion is that these evolutionists have reached positive and final conclusions, but read what Osborn says, page 77, "Men of the Old Stone Age": "We may form our own opinion, however, from a fuller understanding of the specimens themselves, ALWAYS KEEPING IN MIND THAT IT IS A QUESTION WHETHER THE FEMUR (thigh bone) AND THE SKULL (the other piece of bone found as evidence of the "Trinil Race") BELONG TO THE SAME INDIVIDUAL OR EVEN TO THE SAME RACE." If this grave doubt exists, why use the bones as evidence of evolution?

Now look at the facts in this case. The only remains of the now famous Trinil Ape-Man consist of a small section of a skull or brain-pan, two molar or back teeth and a piece of thigh bone unearthed in 1891 near Trinil, Java, by the intimate friend of Ernest Haeckel, Eugene Dubois, a Dutch military surgeon, who described his discovery FOUR YEARS LATER, September 1895, at the Third International Congress of Zoologists at Leyden. One tooth and the piece of skull were found together, the other tooth and the thigh bone together, but about 100 feet from the other bones, within the same year.

Dubois "reconstructed" these remnants, declared they were neither ape nor man, and therefore could only be a connecting link between, naming it "Pithecanthropus Erectus" (ape-man standing upright).

The eminent Prof. Rudolf Virchow, President of the Congress, prudently observed that there was no evidence that the fragments of bone had ever formed part of the same creature, and it was still less possible to characterize such a compound of two creatures either as man or ape, since the thigh bone was evidently human, whereas the fragment of skull certainly belonged to a chimpanzee or a gibbon.

Even Osborn himself admits that the Trinil thigh bone is human and that the Trinil skull-cap is simian. Of the two teeth he says, in "Men of the Old Stone Age," page 81: "They do not resemble those of man closely enough to positively confirm the pre-human theory." Then, why use them to confirm it?

Professor Schwalbe, often quoted by Osborn in support of other phases of evolution, says, "Vorgeschichte des Menschen," 1904, page 29: "The Pithencanthropus Erectus (Trinil Ape-Man) has no place in the genealogical line of man's direct ancestors."

Osborn holds that man's pedigree is not directly related to either living or fossil apes, but to some unknown and undiscovered species. He produces Pithecanthropus as our ancestor. Unfortunately for him, his own witnesses, Professors Schwalbe, Klaatsch and Alsberg, firmly believe Pithecanthropus to be on the same genealogical line as the modern ape. If these authorities are correct, man and the Trinil monstrosity are not on the same family tree, and we are absolutely lost in a maze of contradictions.

Osborn, in spite of the fact that he has produced the Trinil Ape-Man as a "missing link" in No. 1 of his wonderful series of reconstructions, says, in "Men of the Old Stone Age," page 79: "There are, however, reasons for excluding Pithecanthropus from the direct ancestral line of the higher races of man." Of course there are many reasons for exclusion, but none for inclusion.

If he really believes what he has written, why in the name of common-sense, does he place in Case No. 1 eleven skulls and "reproductions," the five on the right being those of gibbon, orang-outang, chimpanzee, adult gorilla, and young gorilla, while the five on the left are reconstructed models of the exploded Piltlown, the mutilated Neanderthal, the shattered Talgai, the reconstructed Cro-Magnon, and a recent human skull? And WHY does he place in a specially made niche and exactly in the center of these two groupes, the more than doubtful bust of the Trinil Ape-Man as a missing link?

He does not say he has ever seen the Trinil Ape-Man. He does not say he knows where his remains are to be found for inspection, or whether they still exist, although they have been discovered for thirty years. He does know that scientists are not permitted to examine them or even to see them. Knowing about all this secrecy, why does he not refer to it?

Dr. Ales Hrdlicka, curator of the United States National Museum, was not allowed to examine or even to see them, and writes in Smithsonian Publication 2300, page 10: "It would surely seem proper and desirable that specimens of such value to science should be freely accessible to well qualified investigators, and that accurate casts be made available to scientific institutions, particularly after twenty (now thirty) years have elapsed since the discovery of the original.

"Regrettable, however, all that has thus far been furnished to the scientific world is a cast of the skull-cap, the commercial replicas of which yield measurements DIFFERENT FROM those reported taken of the original, and several not thoroughly satisfactory illustrations; no reproductions can be had of the femur and the teeth, and not only a study but even a view of the originals are denied to scientific men."

Why, then, does Professor Osborn speak as if he has seen, examined and measured them? Why the queer drawings instead of photographs? Why the significant silence as to these important and mysterious discrepancies?

And so the Trinil Ape-Man as a missing link fades from our view, an elusive phantom, an imaginary conception erected to support a hypothetical and utterly untenable idea as to the origin of man.

(II.) THE HEIDELBERG MAN

Professor Osborn says of this that it represents "a race which was perhaps the predecessor of the Neanderthal man in Europe." It is also described as "a precious document of man's evolution," being known also as the "Mauerjaw," because discovered near the village of Mauer in the Elsenz Valley, about six miles southeast of Heidelberg, by two laborers Oct. 21, 1907. It is preserved in the Palaeontological Institute of Heidelberg University. While featured as the largest jaw thus far discovered, it has well-preserved and unquestionably human teeth.

In "Men of the Old Stone Age," page 100, we read: "It would seem that in the jaw and probably in all other characters of the skull(?) as they became known(?), the Heidelberg race (?) will be found to be a Neanderthal in the making, that is, a primitive, more powerful and more ape-like ancestral form."

And again: "The true Neanderthals rank exactly half way (?) between the most inferior races of man and the anthropoid apes * * * The discovery affords us one of the great missing links or types in the chain of human development."

There is an impressiveness in this confident assertion until we learn that there is no skull with this lower jaw, which was discovered 79 feet below the surface. How, then, can we hope to know any of its "other characters," which seem to give encouragement to the learned Professor?

Dr. Ales Hrdlicka, discussing this specimen in "The Most Ancient Skeletal Remains of Man," page 23, removes the last vestige of hope when he states: "There can be but little hope that other parts of the same skull or skeleton will ever be discovered."

Much discussion has arisen over the comparatively small teeth belonging to this massive Heidelberg jaw, but out interest is lessened when we know that Professor Birkner, in the collection of the Munich Institute for Papaentology, exhibits a modern Eskimo skull in which exactly the same features occur. Has Prof. Osborn overlooked the existence of this modern Eskimo jaw?

We really must repudiate the "precious" Heidelberg "document of man's evolution" as having any claim to being a "Missing link," since it turns out to be nothing more than a large Eskimo lower jaw. Exit, Heidelberg!

(III.) THE GIBRALTAR MAN

is the next "reconstruction" to be studied for a moment. As usual, feeble and barren speculations are called "facts," and by sklilfully avoiding the many embarrassing difficulties which present themselves, Osborn concludes (page 217, "Men of the Old Stone Age") that: "The type skull of this great extinct race of men is that of Neanderthal, appreciated by Lydell and Huxley, but passed over by Darwin, and

112

finally established by Schwalbe as the most important missing link between the existing species of modern man and the anthropoid apes." Again there is no doubt, no hesitation! But even a superficial scrutiny exposes the lamentable deficiencies of this Gibraltar skull.

It is now preserved in the Museum of the Royal College of Surgeons, England, but no one knows anything concerning its history. It was first mentioned in Falconer's "Palaeontological Memoirs," published 1868. Even Prof. Osborn, quoting Dr. Hrdlicka, admits that "No record exists of the precise circumstances under which this interesting relic was found. It was yielded by the rocks many years since."

This is characteristically indefinite, but Prof. Keith, relying on Professor Broca, who recorded absolutely no facts of the discovery of the Gibraltar skull, if he ever knew them, thinks it was taken out from a "very compact and adherent gangue" in Forbes quarry on the north bank of the rock of Gibraltar, as early as 1848. Really, no one knows in what year it appeared, for the reason that nobody paid any attention to it until many years afterwards.

Prof. Osborn, in "Men of the Old Stone Age," page 216, says he doesn't know where the skull was found, and that although its age cannot be determined, it probably belonged to the Mousterian period. He really might have guessed anything as well as that. And yet in the same book, he declares with certainty that the Gibraltar skull was discovered in 1848 by Lieutenant Flint. He further says that the face and base of the cranium are remarkably complete. This is true of the base, but the face is sadly defective, in fact there is no lower jaw and the upper jaw is largely absorbed.

The skull is very small. Keith gives it a capacity of 1100 c. c., 225 c. c. less than the average modern white woman. Dr. Hrdlicka, in "The Most Ancient Skeletal Remains of Man," page 25, says: "There is a marked and quite heavy supraorbital (over the eye) arch." Osborn, on the other hand, speaks of "the slight development of the supraorbital ridges and the small size of the brain."

But, on page 217 of "The Men of the Old Stone Age," Osborn persists in saying: "It is finally established by Schwalbe as the most important missing link between the existing species of modern man and the anthropoid apes." Upon what he bases this statement, neither he nor anyone else has anywhere disclosed.

(IV.) THE NEANDERTHAL MAN

A piece of bone was found August, 1856, by two laborers digging in a small cave at the entrance of Neanderthal Gorge, Westphalia, Germany. Dr. Fhlrohtt became interested and collected a well-preserved human thigh bone, several human arm bones, not so well preserved, fragments of a right arm and forearm bone, a fragment of a human right shoulder blade, a small piece of a human right collar bone, and five broken pieces of rib.

All sorts of legends began to develop around these Neanderthal bones, and among others was one which made them belong to a period in which the latest animals of the Diluvian period still existed, representing a peculiar and hitherto unknown type of ancient humanity, a very close relative to modern man, but "equally close to some preexisting ape now extinct," that is, close to something of which nothing existed. An age was given to this race, ranging from 30,000 years to hundreds of thousands, just as one might prefer.

Even Prof. Schaffhausen admitted 60 years ago: "No proof of this assumption nor consequently of their so-termed fossil condition was afforded by the circumstances under which the bones were discovered."

Virchow and many others considered the bones to be diseased specimens.

From time to time similar skulls were found in different parts of Europe, and it was not long before the claim was made that it was a hitherto unknown type of humanity. For obvious reasons, the capacity of the skull must be placed low, midway between brute and man—between 600

c. c. and 1500 c. c., accordingly Prof. Schaffhausen called it 1033 c. c. Prof. Huxley was forced to correct this estimate and gave it a capacity of 1230 c. c.

Professor Osborn, in his exhibit now presenting unsupported opinions as established fact in the Hall of the Age of Man, describes the Neanderthal race as the "missing link." He labels Case 3, "the immediate predecessor of modern man, the Neanderthal race," notwithstanding the ever-growing body of evidence that the Neanderthals were a race of blacks. He also includes in his Neanderthal circle the cast of a skull discovered at Spy, Belgium; casts of fragments of jaws from Malarnaud, France; fragments of a jaw from Krapina, Croetia; cast of a skull found at Le Moustier, France; cast of a skull from LaChapelle-Aux-Saints, France; "reconstructions" of a female skull found at Gibraltar, 1848 (already considered), including half of the soft parts of the head and a lower jaw restored from studies of ten other Neanderthal jaws.

Would it not be prudent and fair to inform the young and enthusiastic student of anthropology that there are now twelve complete opinions regarding the original Neanderthal skull? The original Neanderthal man has been variously described as an idiot, a Mongolian Cossack, an early German, an early Dutchman, an early Frieslander, a relative of the Australian blacks, a palaeolithic man, a primitive ape-man, etc., etc.

Would it not be honest to show that the outlines of the sagittal, median curve, drawn with Lissaeur's diograph by Macnamara, are almost identical with the skull of the modern Australian black?

Professor Rudolf Virchow is very clear in his statements. He says: "We may certainly regard it as decided that the brain-cast bears no resemblance to that of an ape, and even if the cranium is admitted to be a typical race-cranium, which I consider quite unjustifiable, it does not by any means follow that we may deduce from this that it approximates to that of an ape." An ape—remember, that does not now exist and of which no single trace has ever been found.

Even Professor Schaafhausen declared in his "Der Neanderthal Fund," page 49: "In making this discovery we have not found the missing link between man and the brute."

Professor Macnamara, in "Archiv fur Anthropologie," xxviii., pages 349-360, states that "modern science is compelled to conclude that the Neanderthal skulls do not represent a distinct species of man and cannot therefore be looked upon as missing links, but must be classified as within the limits of variations of the species Homo Sapiens."

Professor Gorjanovic Kramberger, quoted by Prof. Osborn, proves conclusively that modern science cannot and must not regard the Neanderthals and modern man as two distinct species, but merely two races of one and the same species. He says, "Biolog, Zentralblatt," page 810: "It is perfectly plain that the human remains hitherto discovered (referring to all the supposed Neanderthal specimens) all belong to one and the same species * * * proved by the numerous remains found at Krapina, which present many of the characteristics of modern man * * * * proved also by many peculiarities that recur—at the present day. There are now larger jaws than the largest lower jaw found at Krapina. We still meet with broad, square dental arches, badly developed chins, and among the Australian blacks genuine supraorbital ridges."

How much nonsense has been written around these supraorbital ridges which give the beetling brows and the ferocious appearance to the fanciful "reconstructions" of the missing links connecting the ape with modern man?

Even Prof. Arthur Keith says: "We are compelled to admit that men of modern type had been in existence long before the Neanderthal type."

Professor Dwight, of Harvard, says: "For my part I believe the Neanderthal man to be a specimen of a race not arrested in its upward climb, but thrown down from a higher position." This is degeneration from a higher level, not ascending evolution.

It surely is not necessary to spend further time on this exploded "missing link." The greatest authorities in the world have repudiated it. Get in line, Prof. Osborn.

(V.) THE RHODESIA MAN

At the November meeting of the Zoological Society, London, 1921, with Professor McBride, F. R. S., a vice-president of the Society, in the chair, the recently discovered and already famous Rhodesian cave man's skull, christened Homo Rhodesiensis by Dr. Arthur Smith Woodward, F. R. S. (Keeper of Geology at the National History Museum) was the object of discussion. It was announced that experts—unnamed—had given this "ape-like human" an age of 100,000 years. The public was informed that it may now be certain of its monkey origin.

Dr. Woodward stated as his opinion that "Homo Rhodesiensis is decidedly a new link in the chain of evloution, and may prove to be the next grade after the Neanderthal man in the ascending series."

Despite the pronounced simian insinuations of the learned Doctor's remarks, in referring to the "immense size of the palate" of the Rhodesian skull, he admitted that it is "Nevertheless entirely human and beautifully domed—comparable with what we find in modern men, even singers. There is nothing to suggest abnormality." And yet he continues: "As far as I can judge at present, the Rhodesian skull is that of a later man than the Neanderthal man." How then, may we ask, could it have been 100,000 years old?

Professor Elliot Smith, another eminent authority, in discussing this specimen, gives utterance to a grotesque succession of imaginings and suppositions—eight in one paragraph! "Judged by the limbs alone, we would assume that we are dealing with a much more recent type than the Neanderthal man, but judging by the face we would imagine we are dealing with a much older type. As to the sex of the Rhodesian skull, there is the suggestion that it belonged to a woman in the prime of life. The sutures suggest that she was probably less than thirty years of age. When the face was clothed with flesh, I think it might have had widely-splayed nostrils like the gorilla, and in this respect it might have been less like a modern human being than might appear from the skull."

Rhodesia, named after Cecil Rhodes, is a British possession in South Central Africa, lying within the tropics. All the evidence indicates that this entire section of the world was once inhabited by black men, not white, and it may reasonably be inferred therefore that the skull of the Rhodesian cave man is the skull of a black.

The attempt made by some writers to create the impression that the skull was found more than 100 feet below the ground, suggests that the Rhodesian man was buried under successive sedimentary deposits, a fact, which if true, would lend weight to the theory that he was very old.

These are the circumstances. The remains were found in a cave by native laborers, who brought the bones to their overseer, a white man, and then went back to their digging. The facts are reported by William Harris, who was at the mine at the time of the discovery. Some time later, Ross Macartney, the managing director of the Broken Hill mine, gave orders to stop work at that part of the mine and a systematic search for other specimens was made. In addition to the original bones there were found a clavicle (collar bone), a fragment of a scapula (shoulder blade), and a piece of coccyx joined to several sacral vertebrae (base of the spine).

Also, many animal bones were discovered with the human skull and the other human bones—bones of the lion, hyena, elephant, rhinoceros, horse, antelope, gnu, etc.—all modern species.

They also picked up many stone implements, such as the pestle and millstone for grinding grain, implements exactly like those which the African bushman uses today.

It is true the Rhodesian skull was found in a cave, the roof of which had at one time been more than 100 feet thick. Had it been a thousand feet thick instead of 100 it would have made little difference to the Rhodesian man who tumbled through a cleft in the roof, except for the bump at the end of the fall.

What were the pestle and millstone doing in the cave? They must have been used by the men who lived at that time, and the suggestions involved can hardly be reconciled to the habits of life of any pre-historic, ferocious ape-man classically pictured by Professor Knight in The Hall of Man, as a killer armed with a murderous club.

How explain the other certainly human bones found alongside? Is it unreasonable to conclude that they all belong to the same period and are all human?

Contradicting Professor Woodward, Professor G. Elliot Smith declares that "the Rhodesian man is a half-developed Neanderthal man." Dr. Woodward states that he "is decidedly a new link—the next grade after the Neanderthal man in the ascending series."

In the Atlantic Monthly, April, 1922, G. Elliot Smith not only puts the ape-man of Java and the Piltdown of England into respectable society as genuinely unblemished missing links, but he refers also to "the fossil man of Rhodesia," as possessing a face "more definitely primitive and brutal than that of any other human being, living or extinct, that is at present known. The enormous eyebrow ridges are bigger, even than those of the most archaic member of the human family, the Javan Ape-Man; and in the extent and form of their lateral extensions, they recall the condition found in man's nearest simian relative, the gorilla. The nose of the Rhodesian man was definitely more ape-like than that of Neanderthal man."

There are many facts which glaringly refute the missing-link theory. There is not only nothing in the bone deposits to suggest great age, but there is much to indicate that the

Rhodesian man or woman fell into the heap at a comparatively recent date.

Even Professor Smith himself says: "The cleft (in the roof the the cave) does leave open the possibility of the human beings having fallen into the cave at a more recent period."

The evidence is overwhelming as to the recent origin of the Rhodesian skull. None of the human bones are fossilized, although all the bones of the modern animals found with them are completely fossilized. This fossilization must have taken place at a rapid rate on account of the immediate proximity and abundance of extremely active salts of zinc.

The fact that the human skull is not in the least fossilized proves conclusively that the human bones got into the cave at a very much later date than the bones of the modern animals among which it was discovered.

All the other human bones present no extraordinary features, and the skull itself exhibits some very modern characteristics. The teeth are badly decayed, but dental decay is unknown among the palaeolothic Europeans. The opening in the back of the skull is exactly like that of modern man, so situated as to assure an upright position to the head without any forward inclination, such as is the distinctively brutish characteristic of ALL apes, without exception.

The third molar tooth, as with modern man, is notably smaller than the second. The thickness of the skull does not differ from the European skull of 1923. The palate is entirely human, well adjusted for articulate speech.

The eyebrow ridges are indeed heavy, and the slope of the forehead is not exactly normal, but these features are far from proving that the possessor was in any way a "missing link."

The Rhodesian cave man was undoubtedly an African black who fell into the cave of the Broken Hill mine through the cleft in the roof, carrying his implements with him. The same fate met many other men and many modern animals as well. This link in the evolutionary chain proves to be a very weak one and our search remains unrewarded. But we shall persist, and will now examine another bit of evidence (?)

(VI). PILTDOWN MAN

This is No. 2 of the four specimens in the four glass cases in the Hall of the Age of Man, American Museum of Natural History, New York.

As exhibited to the uninitiated the Piltdown man is half ape, half man, but an examination of the facts of the discovery of the few bones from which this "reconstruction" is made by the exercise of a curious and credulous imagination, will show the great weakness of this "link."

Walking along a farm road close to Piltdown Common, Fletching (Sussex), Mr. Charles Dawson "noticed that the road had been mended with some peculiar brown flints not usual in the district." On inquiry he was "astonished" to learn that they had been dug from a gravel bed on the farm. Dawson's statements are somewhat vague, but it would appear that the "discovery" and the "astonishment" occurred sometime in 1909 or 1910, although it was not until December 18th, 1912, that he revealed his find.

On a subsequent visit, a laborer handed him a small portion of unusually thick human parietal bone that looked as if it "might be" 300,000 years old. On another later occasion, in the autumn of 1911, he picked up another and larger piece of bone belonging to the frontal region of a skull, including a portion of the ridge extending over the left eyebrow.

Mr. Dawson took the bones to Dr. A. Smith Woodward of the British Museum. After much talk, a systematic search was made among the heaps of gravel, and the total results consisted of another small piece of occipital bone from the skull, a piece of a jaw bone and a canine or dog tooth.

With these few fragments, the scientists "reconstructed" the Piltdown man and at once proclaimed it to be a new genus which they proceeded to call Eoanthropus or "Dawn Man," naming the species "Dawsoni" in honor of the discoverer.

To make the thing sensational it was necessary to manufacture a "reconstruction" with as close a resemblance to the ape as possible. The nearer to the brute, the more convincing as "scientific evidence" in support of the "missing link" theory.

The skull, of course, must have a capacity midway between that of the ape, 600 c. c., and that of a human, 1500 c. c. According Dr. A. Smith Woodward and Mr. Charles Dawson made their calculations and gave to their Piltdown man a brain capacity, very accurately and very precisely fixed at 1070 c. c.

In August, 1913, when the Piltdown fragments had increased by two molar teeth and two nasal bones, the British Association for the Advancement of Science held its annual meeting. At this gathering Professor Arthur Keith, curator of the Museum of the Royal College of Surgeons, London, shattered the hopes of the evolutionists by demonstrating that the brain capacity of the Piltdown skull was nearer 1500 c. c., than 1070 c. c.

Following this exposure, Professors McGregor and Woodward proceeded to create some new "reconstructions," so that Mr. Piltdown's cranium is now estimated by them at approximately 1300 c. c. But this figure is much too far from 600 c. c. to be comfortable for the argument, and they must somehow give the Piltdown freak an ape-like face and jaw. So the solitary canine tooth is placed very conveniently on the right side of the lower jaw at an angle suggestive of the ape.

But now along come Professor W. K. Gregory and Professor G. S. Miller, writing respectively in the American Museum Journal, vol. 14, 1914, pages 189-200, and Smithsonian Misc. Coll., vol. 65, No. 12, Nov., 1915, proving

122

that the tooth described and used as the right lower canine, was no lower tooth of any kind, and not even a right tooth, but a left tooth and an upper one at that! Alas! Alas! the Piltdown "missing link" is slipping badly.

Professor Ales Hrdlicka, writing in the Smithsonian report for 1913, pages 491-552, re-published by the Government Printing Office, Washington, D. C., 1916, throws us into a new pit of confusion and chaos. He says: "The most important development in the study of the Piltdown remains is * * * the jaw and tooth belong to a fossil chimpanzee."

This is a heartbreaking admission, concurred in by no less an eminent authority than Professor Gerrit S. Miller of the United States National Museum, both scientists urging that none of the conclusions regarding the Piltdown man should be accepted, and that all hypotheses relating to it must be regarded as more or less premature.

No wonder the great German anatomist, G. Schwalbe, so frequently quoted by Professor Osborn, had to abandon the "missing link" opinion so picturesquely and noisily voiced as a scientific fact when he declared that "the proper restoration of the Piltdown fragments would make them belong, not to any preceding stage of man, but to a well developed, good sized Homo Sapiens, the true man of today."

Among many noted scientists who have repudiated the Piltdown "missing link," special mention may be made of Sir Ray Lankester, one of the most distinguished English authorities; Professor David Waterston of the University of London, Kings College; Professor W. D. Matthew of the American Museum of Natural History; and Professor George Grant MacCurdy of Yale University, who wrote in Science, February 18, 1916, page 228-231, of the humiliating Piltdown exposure, referring to the thing as a creature "robbed of a muzzle that ill became him."

Why are these facts not given to the public by the men who persist in labelling this monstrosity a "missing link?" Why do they not tell us the truth, that the Piltdown skull is clearly a human one beneath which the evolutionists have modelled the face of a chimpanzee and so, according to Professor Keith, produced "an impossible animal that could neither breathe nor eat."

Why not tell us about the scientists of world renown who have laughed at this enormous fabrication—men like Professor H. Klaatsch, recognized and quoted in other matters by Prof. Osborn; Professor Hertwig, Professor MacNamara; the great paleontologist Branco, director of the Geological and Paleontological Institute of Berlin University?

Why not give us the opinion of the great Professor Virchow, who declared that "the man-ape has no existence and the missing link remains a phantom?"

(VII.) SUMMARY

Little remains to be said on this subject. Professor Osborn proves by his own table of successive "discoveries" that he is conscious not merely of confusion, but also of misstatement. Mentioning seventeen discoveries in chronological order from 1848 to 1914, he says: "Some of these are now recognized as missing links between the existing human species and the anthropoid apes."

Of the seventeen discoveries ten are Neanderthal. But these, he says, are not missing links. Therefore we must find the missing links among the remaining seven discoveries.

One of the remaining seven is the Trinil Ape-Man, whose ignominous collapse has been dealt with. One of the remaining six is the exploded Piltdown man. This leaves but five discoveries, one of which is the Heidelberg jaw.

Of this Heidelberg jaw Osborn himself says, page 99, "Men of the Old Stone Age": "It is absolutely certain that these remains are human. They show no trace of being intermediate between man and the anthropoid ape."

This Heidelberg jaw must then be discarded as one of the discoveries called "missing links." But Osborn himself repudiates it in one breath and accepts it in the next. He says: "We may consider the Heidelberg jaw as pre-Neanderthaloid."

Now, the Neanderthals and pre-Neanderthals must be human beings—true men, or they must be missing links connecting true men with apes. In one sentence Prof. Osborn infers they are one, and in the next the other.

However, as science, regardless of the Professor's confused statement, does not recognize the Heidelberg jaw as a missing link, there are but four other discoveries to justify his vague declaration.

These are two skulls discovered 1867, at Furfooz, Belgium; three skeletons and fragments of two others discovered 1868, and known as the Cro-Magnon, Dordogne; two skeletons discovered 1901, in the Grimaldi Grotto, Mentone; and two skeletons discovered 1914 at Oberkrassel, near Bonn, Germany.

Two of these, the discoveries of 1868 and 1914, are described as "comparatively modern Cro-Magnon true men," and cannot therefore be recognized as missing links.

Of the two specimens left, the Furfooz skulls were discovered by Dupont, 1867, in a cave near Furfooz, in the Valley of the Lesse, Belgium. They are described as a highly developed race of men, whose descendants are the broad-headed races now found in Holland and Denmark. Osborn himself quotes this opinion: ("Men of the Old Stone Age," page 485). Of course he does not refer to the Furfooz skulls as recognized missing links.

There is nothing left, then, but the Grimaldi skeletons of 1901, found in the Grottes de Grimaldi, near Mentone, described as displaying "a number of resemblances to the African negroid race."

Boule is responsible for most of the ideas now in circulation regarding the bones found in the Grimaldi Grotto, which really consist of two sets of remains—one belonging to the African negroid race, the other to the Cro-Magnon race. Since both of these are admitted by evolutionists to be later races than the Neanderthals, we are farther away than ever from the missing link, as without doubt no son could ever have appeared before the birth of his father!

Evidently the reason that Professor Osborn avoids specific mention of a single one of the seventeen discoveries as a missing link, is because there is no missing link among them.

Endeavoring to explain his own contradictions by the use of another group of contradictions of certain "authorities" selected by him, because they seem, unless too closely inspected, to support his own opinions, Professor Osborn, in "Men of the Old Stone Age," page 54, as Arthur Thomson does in "Outline of Science," vol. 1, publishes the ancestral tree of the anthropoid apes and men.

They begin with the "unknown ancestral stock" of the Old World primates, including man, one branch of which leads to the small monkeys of Egypt and the Macaques of Asia and Europe. Another branch became the Propliopithecus, one of whose children was the orang of Asia, another the gorilla of Africa, a third the chimpanzee of Africa, a fourth the gibbon of Asia, and a fifth led to the "Unknown Pliocene ancestors of man," from whom "in the order of descent" are placed the "Trinil Ape-Man," the "Heidelberg Man," the "Piltdown Man," the "Neanderthal Man," more primitive species, human and pre-human, than the "Cro-Magnon" and other races, and finally on top of the tree, Homo Sapiens, meaning you and the the rest of us.

The student who does not examine closely as he looks at that tree, would quickly conclude that the Trinil Ape-Man came out of pure ape; that the Heidelberg man, still very much ape, came out of the Trinil Ape-Man; that the Piltdown man, still very gorilla-like, came out of the Heidelberg man; that the Neanderthal man, with many apish characteristics still clinging to his squat ferocity, came out of the Piltdown man; that other pre-human and human primitives came out of the Neanderthal man; that the Cro-Magnon and more highly developed races came out of these primitive sub-men, and that in turn, out of the Cro-Magnon cave man, who was an improvement on all the others, came modern man.

Our study proves that nothing is further from the truth than these strange but momentous conclusions. According to the evolutionist, everyone may grow his own family ancestral tree. Each may become his own modeller, and depending entirely upon his skill in art, may manufacture his own "reconstructions," but in doing so must forever ignore the irrefutable evidence of contemporary races.

Otherwise his series of "progressive" stages breaks down and his connecting links are lost. Above all, he must avoid candor and truth and abandon reason.

Everything must begin with what is described as the "unknown," as far as paleontology is concerned. Everything may end according to the formula of H. G. Wells, who, in his "Outline of History," takes what is unknown, labels it "known," and then tells the world this is "advanced science," "stripped of all superstition, mysticism, theology and other nonsense!"

H. G. Wells is suffering from "the blind staggers of science," as anyone must who indulges in the sort of reasoning that he adopts. That this so-called "science" has appropriated so much self-certified dignity, and has fooled so many "educated" men, will ever remain one of the mysteries of this ouija-board age.

The reader who has travelled thus far through the inextricably confused "missing link" jumble which science has presented to us, and which science itself is unable to unravel, because of the complicated, involved, corrupted and contradictory opinions of scientists writing on the subject—knows all that H. G. Wells ever knew or ever could know concerning these paleontological specimens.

A consideration of the conclusions of Wells, Osborn, Thomson, and many others, presented white-hot in the name of stone-cold science, shows that "science" has become, through the betrayal of its own high priests, the plaything of romancers, novelists, and mountebanks.

SCIENCE SPEAKS TO OSBORN

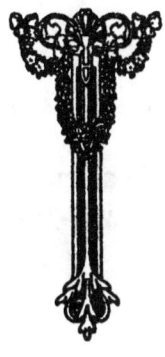

BY

Arthur I. Brown, M.D., C.M., F.R.C.S.E.

Copyrighted 1927
by
GLAD TIDINGS PUBLISHING CO.
Fort Wayne, Indiana

SCIENCE SPEAKS TO OSBORN

Arthur I. Brown, M.D., C.M., F.R.C.S.E.

After reading Henry Fairfield Osborn's book, "The Earth Speaks to Bryan," 1925, one is inclined to agree with the verdict of William James in his "Life and Letters," vol. II, pg. 220. He writes:

> "Of all insufficient authorities as to the total nature of reality, give me the scientists from Munsterburg up, or down. Their interests are most incomplete and their professional conceit and bigotry immense. I know no narrower sect or club."

In this book of Osborn's we look for facts but discover only foolishness. We expect valid evidence, but find nothing but empty words. Osborn not only places himself on a pedestal, high and far removed from his brother scientists, on whom he looks down from his lofty intellectual isolation with condescension, as he interprets Science for them, but he actually presumes to speak for God Himself.

He scorns John Burroughs, the great naturalist, because he has written a strong and convincing but "wholly misleading article" on natural selection. He anathematizes the distinguished biologist, William Bateson, who was undoubtedly without a superior in the world, in his special field. Osborn says that "he is living the life of a scientific specialist out of the main current of biological discovery and that his opinion that we have failed to discover the origin of species is valueless and directly contrary to the truth."

He explains further that biologists find it "difficult to think straight on this very intricate subject of Evolution", but, of course, no branch of science presents any mysteries to the president of the American Museum of Natural History!

Think of it! Men, conceded by the world to be in the front rank of scientific investigation, cannot speak with any authority even in their own specialty, if these opinions happen to disturb the dogmatic and false conclusions of this blinded, dyed-in-the-wool evolutionist! It is amusing.

With a multitude of complacent and confident generalities he endeavors to bludgeon into unconscious and servile submission those who attempt to think for themselves on this question.

With him, as with so many evolutionary devotees, "Romance and Speculation have seized the reins from Reason and Science and are running amuck in the realm of absurd and illogical supposition."

With an impertinent arrogance unsurpassed in the history of scientific dogmatism, he hurls his offensive diatribes at any and all who dare to stand in his path. He exhibits the most colossal degree of ignorant and blind egotism, masquerading under the guise of sound science and scholarly attainment, that the world has witnessed in this generation.

Not only does he ignore or reject factual objective evidence beyond the possibility of contradiction, but he deliberately distorts and misrepresents his quotations, making the writers responsible for thoughts and opinions never expressed, and conclusions diametrically opposed to the truth as they see it.

His statements are so far removed from fact and so grotesquely denied by evidence available to everyone, that the only conclusion is that this author assumes that his word will pass unquestioned and that his readers are either unable or unwilling to read and think for themselves.

The time has passed when offensive snobbery and ill-mannered personal abuse are satisfactory substitutes for legitimate argument. Those who are now studying evolution, want, and will insist on getting facts. They refuse to accept Prof. Osborn at his own valuation. This is a heinous offense, but we shall risk the penalty of excommunication from the ranks of the "intelligentia", and consignment to the bottomless depths of that region of darkness inhabited by ignorant and obscurantist opponents of the "law of evolution". The deadly shrapnel discharged in our direction has proved to be nothing more than a collection of harmless squibs.

Osborn admits that he will "not enter into the well-known details of the wonderful processes of evolution as they have been constantly observed in plants and animals for a century and a half". He is wise not to attempt the impossible, but we shall insist on a little discussion of these essential "wonderful processes". We want to know—not the conclusions of the evolutionists—but the facts on which they base their belief. We are well able—yes, quite as well able as they—to make reasonable decisions on the points at issue.

This author is so busy squirming under the embarrassing and painful attacks of Bryan, whose arguments he finds wholly unanswerable, that the only weapon left to him is cheap and futile ridicule. Like many other critics he is sufferng from an acute and incurable form of "Bryanitis". He confesses that he is "deeply impressed with the fact that Bryan has familiarized himself with many of the debatable points in Darwin's opinions". Well, that is something! We would almost believe sometimes that Bryan could neither read nor write, had been blind and deaf from birth, but, strangely, was able to speak fairly well. As a matter of fact, Bryan had been such a diligent student of evolution and its absurdities that, like many other intelligent men and women, he has decided it was time a bit of light was let in on the situation. We know that he was a constant thorn in the flesh of the evolutionists, who prefer darkness to light. Their constant trick is to go back uncounted millions of centuries for their evidence and into the unseen and inaccessible depths of the earth. There the scientific imagination can wander at will in a maze of idle speculation, with little danger of contradiction (they think), and apparently with much pleasure, if not edification, to themselves.

The title of this book, "The Earth Speaks to Bryan," indicates that he appeals to geology. Therefore, unto geology we shall go. We shall see whether the message of the earth to Bryan and the rest of us, sustains or destroys evolution. We shall discover whether it is an accepted "law" or a grotesque and impossible theory.

—6—

134

We will not allow anyone, Osborn included, to establish for himself a criterion of criticism different from that applied to any other branch of science. Much as he desires it, we cannot place him in the position of supreme eminence where his wildest statements will neither be questioned nor investigated. We shall apply reason and common sense to certain of his specific claims.

Osborn, and many of the smaller fry who follow in his train, are very fond of high-sounding declaration as to the "assured results of modern research," and constantly remind us that evolution has passed from the realm of theory to that of fact. But we confess to grave suspicions on this point.

Osborn writes:

> "The evolution of higher and lower forms of life is as well and as soundly established as the eternal hills. It has long ceased to be a theory; it is a law of nature as universal in living things as is the law of gravitation in material things and in the motion of the heavenly spheres."

These are strong words. Are they justified? Let other world-renowned scientists be heard,—men whose opinion cannot be ignored or repudiated with a shrug of the shoulders as of no consequence.

Dr. Fink, professor of anatomy in Berlin University, recently said, as quoted by the "Allgemeine Evangelische Lutherische Kirchenzeitung":

> "It must be clearly recognized that there are no facts at the base of the evolutionary theory. It is purely a theory and in no case should it be erected into a dogma."

Similar opinions could be multiplied indefinitely. There are few individuals so perfectly satisfied with the character of the proof of the evolutionary hypothesis as Henry Fairfield Osborn.

Paul Kammerer of Vienna, until his recent death by suicide, a leading evolutionist, wrote in the "Literary Review," February 23, 1924, p. 528:

> "The theory of evolution at the present time is returning to the theory of non-evolution."

Osborn expresses his implicit faith in natural selection, but here he is opposed by the great majority of modern transformists, such as Vernon Kellogg, William Bateson, T. H. Morgan, Locke, Willis, Tansley, Cunningham, McMurrick, James Harvey Robinson and many others whose very positive utterances could be given if space permitted it.

James Harvey Robinson summed up the situation in Harper's magazine of June, 1924, in an article, "Is Darwinism Dead?" He shows that modern science has repudiated Darwin's ideas of natural selection and survival of the fittest. He wrote:

> "If Darwin were alive he would be the first to confess that his explanations have little or no value today."

Can it be possible that Professor Osborn himself is so "outside the main current of scientific thought," that he has not heard the voices of earth, sea and sky, speaking loudly, in clarion tones, of the decline and death of Darwin's conceptions, to which he clings so tenaciously and so blindly?

He is very certain indeed that the rock record of the fossils prove the gradual progression in the development of life-forms over many millions of years. He says:

> "To sum up the testimony of the rocks, the evidence as regards the creative evolution of man is as unanswerable as that of the creative evolution of the entire plant and animal world. Man is no exception to the universal law that God did use evolution as His plan."

It would seem from this that there is nothing more to be said, but investigation reveals this statement to be far, far from the truth, and to have no foundation in fact. This alleged gradual evolvement of organisms, involving innumerable transformations of species from lower to higher forms, is not supported by any evidence in Nature. Other scientists, at least equally qualified, deny this dogmatic assertion of Osborn's.

Professor Adam Sedgwick, British embryologist, writing in the Encyclopedia Britannica on "Embryology," quotes, with approval, Huxley's statement:

> "An impartial survey of positively ascertained truth negatives the common doctrine of progressive modification or a necessary progression from more or less embryonic form. It either shows us no evidence of any such modification or demonstrates it to be very slight."

Professor Osborn says that:

> "The wondrous lines of ascent invariably follow the principle of creative evolution whereby the simple and more lowly forms always precede the higher and more specialized forms."

He goes on to point out the beautifully graded progression from the lowly amoeba, to tadpole, and to water-breathing fish, from which arises the air-breathing amphibian. From the water-living amphibian comes the land-living, air-breathing reptile, and from the latter, two lines leading to bird and mammal, respectively. And then he remarks facetiously, "This is not perhaps the way Bryan would have made the animals but this is the way God made them." And that's that! Being on intimate terms with the Creator of the universe, this twentieth-century super-man can speak with the utmost authority! And we read further:

"As for the creative evolution of man, passing by the early speculative writings of such men as Haeckel, we now have more than a dozen substantial volumes based not upon guesswork or speculation but upon the testimony yielded in the superficial layers of the earth and in caves, embracing hundreds of specimens of the fossilized remains of man, more or less ancient, more or less complete, but invariably, without a single exception, testifying to the gradual ascent of man from a lower to a higher state, gradually dropping one primitive bit of anatomy after another until the high, intelligent, fully human aspect is attained."

"Again with clarion voice these irrefutable witnesses of our past positively demonstrate two new and somewhat unexpected truths: first, that man has not descended from any known kind of monkey or ape, fossil or recent; with this truth, established not by Bryan but by the testimony of the earth, one of the chief sentimental objections to the creative evolution of man disappears forever. Second, man has a long independent, superior line of ascent of his own, with a relatively erect posture, with hands free to grasp and use tools, with thumb and fore-finger capable of handling flint implements, such as the graving tools and brush of the artist, and finally, the reed, pen, or crayon, with which to set down his thoughts. Challenge as we may the less perfect discoveries in the Trinil sands, in the Piltdown gravels, in the Heidelberg riverbeds, no man can challenge the convincing testimony to the creative evolution of man afforded by several complete skeletons of the race of the Neanderthal who lived 100,000 years ago, nor the perfectly preserved fossil remains of the artistic race of the Cro-Magnons, who lived 30,000 years ago.

"The Neanderthal hunters of 100,000 years ago and the Cro-Magnon artists of 30,000 years ago are not guesswork or the fabric of scientific imagination; they are realities, men like ourselves, the older one a much lower race—a veritable missing link—the other a higher race with all powers equal to our own."

What is the real truth of the matter? Does Osborn know what he is talking about? Is he mistaken, notwithstanding the positions he holds as research professor of zoology, Columbia University; senior geologist, U. S. Geology Survey; and president American Museum of Natural History? Is he, knowing these statements to be false, determined, at all costs, to discredit the Biblical account of creation? Those who acquaint themselves with the easy available facts may solve the problem.

Is the geological record so complete, so accurate or so convincingly corroborative of the evolutionary theory as he would have us believe? Apparently not. Let us review the present status of fossil evidence and see what value it has. Does it show progressive modifications in life-forms from simple to complex? Are those wonderful "missing links" reliable evidence of man's ascent from animal? What is the "consensus of opinion" to which the evolutionist attaches such tremendous importance? We summon to the witness stand some of the foremost authorities of the world, men who know whereof they speak. Neither Osborn nor anyone else dare ignore them.

Professor Oswald Spengler, one of the greatest thinkers and philosophers of the day, has written one of the most startling books produced in twenty-five years. This massive work bears the title, "Der Untergang des Abendlandes"—"The Decay of the Western World." In vol. II, p. 35, he writes as follows:

> "Our notions regarding the history of the earth's crust and of the various forms of life, are still controlled by the theory of Lyell and of other Englishmen, who stress a slow development extending over long periods, rather than sudden catastrophes, as taught by the great Leopold Von Buch and by Cuvier. The fundamental error of the theory is that it excludes all forms of energy which are not active today. There is no more complete refutation of Darwin than the study of fossils. As far as man is concerned, **the fossil remains prove** that all forms which existed in the past correspond to those living today. **Not the slightest trace of development of the race towards higher structure can be found.**
>
> "**Man** has come as **the result** of **sudden** change, of which the whence, why and how will be an unfathomable mystery. Thus the assumption of enormous periods of time for human development is unnecessary. The most ancient beginnings of Egyptian civilization may well fit into the five thousand years of accepted history. The origin of the earth, the beginning of life,

—12—

the introduction of animated beings, are mysteries which we must accept as such."

Dr. F. A. Bather, M.A., D. Sc., F.R.S., in his presidential address before the geological section of the British Association at Cardiff, Wales, said:

"The Palaeontologist will probably never reveal the root and lower part of the ancestral tree . . . The whole basis of our system is being shifted . . .

"Descent is **not a** corollary of succession . . . History is not the same as evolution. Today we claim to have proved evolution by descent. How do we prove it? The evidence remains circumstantial . . .

"There is, then, reason for thinking that **ignorance alone leads us to assume** some inexplicable force urging the races this way and that to so-called advance or to apparent degeneration, to life or to déath."

Louis T. More, professor of physics, Cincinnati University, in his "The Dogma of Evolution," 1925, pg. 12, writes:

"Science places man in a literal world of law and order and relegates all perturbing perplexities to the incomprehensible background of the immeasurably small or the infinitely great. Life and matter on the earth are the dance of atoms, and atoms are so small that we can forget their variations, and the earth itself is in so vast a universe that its perturbations are negligible . . .

"At first sight, we are impressed by the great quantities of relics which have been retrieved from desolation of the past and have been collected and noted in the many museums established throughout the civilized world. These relics have been studied and classified, both as to character and time, by patient men of science; until they have at last pieced them together as a mosaic and fitted them into a frame of time. We are, for awhile, impressed with the abundance of these evidences of the past history until, with something of a shock, we begin to speculate on the inconceivable number of plant and animal forms which have come and gone. The earth comprises some two hundred million square miles of surface and there is scarcely a portion of it which does not teem with life. And this population has lived and died and been replaced endless times in the hundreds of millions of years which have elapsed since the earth has been cool enough to permit organic life to exist. Of all this multitude of once living things, only a minute portion which possessed calcareous bones or shells, or chanced to have its softer parts petrified, could have left any trace behind it; and only a minute portion of these can ever be accessible to discovery. Then we begin to realize that the display cases before us contain all the organic beings which have been preserved from those which peopled a continent during millions of years. This bone is the sole relic of many genera of animals; and this handful of shells is the recovered remnant of the countless life of the sea during other millions of years. From what we have collected from the past and from observation of forms at present alive, a theory of evolution has been laboriously developed which explains our existing life as the result of a continuous modification of previous forms, going back to simpler and simpler organisms until we reach a world of inorganic matter with here and there tiny masses of protoplasmic jelly scattered on the shores of the ocean, themselves indistinguishable from the mud in which they lie.

—14—

"Yet from these few and wholly inadequate facts, the history of the world, from the time when it was a molten and fiery mass to the present time, is given to us by geologists and biologists. The changing structure of land and sea is traced, the succession of plants and animals is outlined, not in vague and general terms, but specifically from type to type; a table of time is worked out, which, although it may vary in details of a million years here and there, is nevertheless agreed upon in its main groups. The ages of rock strata and of mountains and seas are specified and the changes coincident in organic life are noted. Not only these things are laid down for us to believe, but also the causes of the changes from one type to another are described as matters of scientific verity; even obscure and insignificant habits of men are traced back to the prehistoric traits of our animal forefathers. For example, a baby clings to the finger of its parent because one of its progenitors, as a monkey, clung to the branch of a tree, or, as others hold, we have a curved back and a tottering walk because we have descended from monkeys which were inhabitants of treeless plains, and we have not yet learned to move upright. The biological history which thus not only marks the gigantic steps of time but also descends to a multitude of minute facts and incidents, which occurred millions of years before man with his records inhabited the earth, should have a certain and adequate basis of fact. Does this ground-work of observation and fact exist?'

Professor More answers this question in the negative, and a little further on he writes:

"In spite of this totally inadequate foundation which paleontology offers for a scientific theory of evolution and causes of variation,

there has never been known such a campaign of organized propaganda in the name of science."
And again:

> "The agnosticism towards religion or philosophy, call it which you will, of the Darwinians now embraces the **truths** of their science . . . I have had a pretty severe and long training as a laboratory experimenter. I am quite prepared to accept the conclusions of biological experimentation and shall depend upon the statements of biologists to show that they have not bridged the gap between the organic and inorganic world; that they are not prepared to explain living processes as physical force and energy; that biological evolution as a guide to human society is a delusion."

Then, in regard to the claims of the paleontologist, More devotes fifty pages to show how unwarranted these claims really are. He concludes his article on Geology, pg. 160, by saying:

> "The more one studies paleontology, the more certain one becomes that evolution is based on faith alone; exactly the same sort of faith which it is necessary to have when one encounters the great mysteries of religion. The changes that are noted as time progresses show no orderly and no consecutive evolutionary chain, and, above all, they give us no clue whatever as to the cause of variation."

Now, what did Darwin say? In his "Origin of Species," vol. II, pg. 49, he wrote:

> "Geology assuredly does not reveal any such finely graduated organic chain; and this, perhaps, is the most obvious and serious objection which can be urged against the theory of Natural Selection."

—16—

And listen to Huxley, in his "Biological and Geological Essays," pg. 297:

> "In view of the immense diversity of known animal and vegetable forms and the enormous lapse of time indicated by the accumulation of fossiliferous strata, the only circumstance to be wondered at is not that the changes of life, as exhibited by positive evidence, have been so great, but that they have been so small."

What about these fossil remains supposed to be predecessors of man and to prove that man and his immediate ancestors, half human, half animal, have been on earth for hundreds of thousands of years?

Osborn writes with amazing cocksureness about these long-since-exploded missing links. Apparently he has been enjoying a Rip Van Winkle sleep while the exposures of these dishonest reconstructions have been going on. He swallows all, hook, line and sinker,—Pithecanthropus Erectus (the Trinil Ape Man,) the Piltdown man, the Heidelberg Man, the Neanderthal Man, the Foxhall Man, the Cro-Magnon Man. According to him, their life history is certain for at least half a million years.

But M. de Quatrefages, writing concerning the mythical family tree, universally adopted by Osborn and his friends, declared:

> "Not one of the creatures in this pedigree has ever been seen. No skeleton or fossil of a single one of these creatures has ever been discovered. Their existence is based wholly on theory. To fill his gaps, Haeckel invents types as well as the line of descent to which he assigns them. Whenever a branch or twig is lacking on his genealogical tree, whenever the tran-

sit from one type to another would appear too abrupt he invents species and groups, bodily, to which he unhesitatingly assigns a place.

"Is it not very singular that precisely that evidence must be supposed always to have perished which the evolutionary theory imperatively requires, while so much evidence remains to contradict it?"

Professor A. O. Seward of Cambridge University, tells us in "Nature," April 26, 1924:

"The present tendency is to discard the old-fashioned genealogical tree with its wonderful diversity of branches as not at all a suitable method of picturing the course of organic development. The student who takes an impartial retrospect soons discovers that the 'fossil' record raises more problems than it solves."

It is not necessary to prolong these negative opinions in regard to the evolutionary tree based on the alleged evidence of geology. The claims of Osborn, et al, are not verified by the facts of nature. Nor is it necessary to go into detail in regard to the twelve or thirteen notorious missing links which have been hailed as authentic proof of man's ascent from animal forms. A few remarks on some of them will show how weak is the case for the evolutionist.

Today it is not difficult to find men of eminent scientific attainments who are flatly opposed to evolution in all its forms. One of the most recent examples is George Barry O'Toole, Ph. D., S.T.D., Professor of Theology and Professor Emeritus of Philosophy, St. Vincent Archabbey; Professor of Animal Biology, Seton Hill College, Greensburgh, Pa. His book is a closely-reasoned, logically un-

—18—

answerable argument against evolution, and its title is "The Case Against Evolution" (1925). In the section dealing with "The Origin of the Body" he discusses in considerable detail each of the principal fossil remains in which certain paleontologists profess to see evidence of the transition between man and the primitive pithecoid stock. He shows conclusively that all the alleged connecting links are distinctly human or purely simian, or merely mismated combinations of human and simian remains. He writes about Pithecanthropus Erectus, the Heidelberg Man, the Piltdown Man, the Neanderthal Man No. 1, Neanderthal Man No. 2, the Man of La Naulette, the Man of Spy, the Men of Crapina, the Le Moustier Man, the La Chapelle Man, the Rhodesian Man and the Foxhall Man. His summary of these remains is as follows:

> "Summa Summarum: So far as science knows, only one human species has ever existed on the earth, and that is Homo sapiens. All the alleged connecting links between men and apes are found, on careful examination, illusory. When not wholly ambiguous in view of their inadequate preservation and fragmentary character, they are (as regards both mind and body) distinctly human, like the Neanderthal man, or they are purely simian, like the Pithecanthropus, or they are heterogenous combinations of human and simian bones, like the Eoanthropus Dawsoni (Piltdown Man.) 'With absolute certainty,' says Hugues Obermaier, 'we can only say that man of the Quarternary period differed in no essential respect from man of the present day. In no way did he go beyond the limits of variation of the normal human body.' ("The Oldest Remains of the Human Body, etc.," Vienna, 1905.) The so-called homo primigenius,

therefore, is not a distinct species of human being, but merely an ancient race that is, at most, a distinct variety or subspecies of man. **In spite of tireless searching, no traces of a bestial irrational man have been discovered.** Indeed man, whom nature has left naked, defenseless, unarmed with natural weapons, and deficient in instinct, has no other resources than his reason, and could never have survived without it. To imagine primitive man in a condition analogous to that of the idiot is preposterous. 'For other animals,' says St. Thomas of Aquin, 'Nature has prepared food, garments of fur, means of defense, such as teeth, horns and hoofs, or at least swiftness in flight. But man is so constituted that, none of these things having been prepared for him by nature, reason is given him in their stead, reason by which through his handiwork he is enabled to prepare all these things . . . Moreover, in other animals there is inborn a certain natural economy respecting those things which are useful or hurtful, as the lamb by nature knows the wolf to be its enemy. Some animals also by natural instinct are aware of the medicinal properties of herbs and of other things which are necessary for life. Man, however, has a natural knowledge of these things which are necessary for life only in general, as being able to arrive at the knowledge of the particular necessities of human life by way of inference from general principles.' ("De regim, princ.," 1. I. c. I.) As a matter of fact, **man is never found apart from evidence of his intelligence.** The Neanderthaloid race, with their solemn burials and implements of bone and stone, exemplify this truth no less than the palaeolithic artists of the Cave of Altamira."

Only one or two more points worthy of discussion remain for consideration in this book of Osborn's. This modern scientist seeks support from the ancient Augustine. It is strange that he should desire corroboration from a long past age when scientific opinions were immature and, we have supposed, of no value to the twentieth century wise man. It is stranger still that Osborn should put into the mouth of Augustine, words which he never uttered, and should thus violently distort and misrepresent his opinions. But this is a fact.

Osborn writes of Augustine pp. 25-26:

> "I feel that I may direct Mr. Bryan's attention to a writer whom evidently he has studied; namely, the great theologian of the fifth century, St. Augustine . . . To Augustine, Mr. Bryan may be referred for a sound and thoroughly modern theistic conception of evolution. Augustine held that all development takes its natural course through the powers imparted to matter by the Creator; even the bodily structure of man himself is according to this plan, and therefore a product of this natural development; he taught that in the institution of Nature we should not look for miracles, but for the laws of Nature; he distinctly rejected the Mosaic idea of the six-day creation in favor of the teaching which, without violence to language, we may call a theory of evolution: that all things developed by causal energy and potency, not only the heavens, but also those living things which the waters and the earth produced, so that in due time, after long delays, they developed into their perfected forms."

This statement of Augustine's faith is absolutely contrary to the truth. If anyone had put the question to him that by a law of Nature an ape had descended from a fish, he would have repelled the

—21—

idea as inconceivable; the statement that man came from an ape would have been nothing short of blasphemy. Unfortunately for Mr. Osborn, Augustine has left a clear and full statement of his views. This statement shows that he accepted the Mosiac cosmogony literally, with very few insignificant reservations. Certainly the evolutionist can derive little comfort from his words in his book "The City of God," translated by Rev. Marcus Dods:

> "God, who made the world, has made it so that all things are admirable, and the beauty and order show its divine authorship. If we ask who made it, the answer is God. He also made it out of nothing and He made it because it was good. All things were made in six days as revealed to Moses . . . The human race began with one man whom God placed in Paradise. He was created upright but was corrupted by his own will and begot corrupted and condemned children . . . They are deceived who believe those highly mendacious documents which profess to give the history of many thousand years, when reckoned by the sacred writings not six thousand years have yet passed."

How will Mr. Osborn explain his misquotation? Of course, as he has presumed to speak for the Creator of the Universe, he can much more easily express the correct views of Augustine in spite of the fact that Augustine's words contradict him!

The wild statements regarding the great antiquity of man merit a little notice. The evolutionist deals in millions of years. He is very prodigal of time. In fact, this is absolutely necessary in order to give his theory even a semblance of plausibility.

It may be taken for granted that the opinion of George Frederick Wright, one of the greatest geologists of all time, ought to have some weight. In his "Origin and Antiquity of Man" he sums up his conclusions, pp., 495 and 496:

> "A study of the history of the world reveals the further fact that there has been no marked tendency of improvement in the human race except as it has been brought in contact with the developing civilization that appears in the earliest historical times . . . The history of the human race as we actually know it gives no countenance to any doctrine of universal and general progress among the races of mankind, but sustains rather a doctrine of predominant natural tendencies to degeneration, which is only counteracted by contact with specially favored nations and by voluntary acceptance of their most valuable ideas and practices.
>
> "While the antiquity of man cannot be less than ten thousand it need not be more than fifteen thousand years. Eight thousand years of prehistoric time is ample to account for all known facts relating to his development. That his origin was by divine intervention will be the verdict of most sane and candid minds."

The chronological tables used so freely by orthodox geologists have long been accepted as accurate and beyond dispute. On investigation, however, we discover that these tables have absolutely no value either as showing the age of the earth, the age of the geological strata, the age of the contained fossils, nor of the antiquity of man.

Certainly the palaeontological record furnishes no evidence worthy of the name, that our globe has been a scene of a process of organic evolution. This paper does not deal specifically with the gigantic obstacles in the way of an acceptance of current geological conclusions. Anyone who cares to inform himself on the subject should read "The New Geology" by George McCready Price. Because of his heterodox views and his unanswerable expose of the false palaeontological and evolutionary conclusions, he has suffered excommunication from the ranks of modern so-called scientists. They anathematize him but do not answer his arguments, not because they would not, but because they cannot. George Barry O'Toole in "The Case Against Evolution," pg. 126, says:

> "The Palaeontological argument is simply a theoretical construction which presupposes evolution instead of proving it. Its classic pedigrees of the horse, the camel and the elephant are only credible when we have assumed the 'facts' of evolution, and even then, solely upon condition that they claim to approximate, rather than assign, the actual ancestry of the animals in question.
> "In palaeontology, as in the field of zoology, evolution is not a conclusion, but an interpretation. In palaeontology, otherwise than in the field of genetics, evolution is not amenable to the check of experimental tests, because here it deals not with that which is, but with that which was. Here the sole objective basis is the mutilated and partially obliterated record of a march of events, which no one has observed and which will never be repeated.
> "These obscure and fragmentary vestiges of a vanished past, by reason of their very incompleteness, lend themselves quite readily to all sorts of theories and all sorts of speculations. Of the 'Stone Book of the Universe' we may

say with truth that which Oliver Wendell Holmes says of the privately interpreted Bible, namely, that its readers take from it the same views, which they had previously brought to it: 'I am, however, thoroughly persuaded,' says the late Yves Delage, 'that one is or is not a transformist, not so much for reasons deduced from natural history, as for motives based on personal philosophic opinions. If there existed some other scientific hypothesis besides that of descent to explain the origin of species, many transformists would abandon their present opinion as not being sufficiently demonstrated . . . If one takes his stand upon the exclusive ground of the facts, it must be acknowledged that the formation of one species from another species has not been demonstrated at all.' " ("L'heredite et les grands problems de la biologie generale," Paris, 1903, pp. 204, 322.")

It is too much to hope that the men who are quoted in this article will be considered by the Osborn group in any sense authoritative. The usual procedure of evolutionists when confronted with views contrary to their own dogmatic opinions, is to call their opponents "inconsequential scientists." This, conceivably, may satisfy *them,* but is no answer to the individual seeking for light and truth.

Those who criticize William Jennings Bryan and Fundamentalists generally, are very loud in their denunciation of what they call an insolent attempt to restrict the teaching of science. They prate everlastingly regarding those who believe in an infallible Bible, and who apparently prefer to remain "unenlightened." We are accused of being medieval, of believing the earth to be flat, or rejecting the Copernican theory, and the law of gravitation. If we have not actually so expressed ourselves it is because we still have some regard for the good opinions of our evolutionist friends.

To accept the story of Jonah and the Whale and that the sun stood still at the behest of Joshua; to adopt an unwavering faith in a literal interpretation of the whole Bible, is sufficient evidence to them of our simplicity and gullibility, if not of our positive insanity.

They consider the Bible to be excellent food for our moral and spiritual hunger even though its history is false, and its science crude. The Bible becomes a human collection of deliberate falsehoods, glaring errors and palpable contradictions, the result of a pitiable ignorance. Notwithstanding all these defects, it teaches the sublimest spiritual truths. Since time began, this is surely the first instance of a bad tree bringing forth good fruit! The Word of God is damned with faint praise.

It is held up for our admiration because of its moral and spiritual value, and, at the same time, is anathematized on account of its false and contradictory science. Those who cannot understand how a book can be both morally perfect and historically untrustworthy do not know what feats of legerdemain are possible to modern science!

This incessant flow of grandiose declarations from the tainted evolutionary fountain, and the invariable assumption of all knowledge, by these modernists who adopt such a sneering and condescending attitude towards their opponents, is becoming a trifle wearisome.

—26—

False accusations of ignorance and obscurantism may be permitted as quite harmless, but these claims to infallibility and omniscience really try our forbearance.

Of course, the charge that Fundamentalists desire to restrict the teaching of real science is a herring across the trail for the purpose of hiding the real issue. But Fundamentalists do insist that those teachers supported by the tax-payer should be prevented from teaching as facts these wholly unproven hypotheses of evolution, which are contradicted by all the evidence, and which seek to discredit and dishonor the Bible. Let those parents who wish to have this theory taught to their children, erect schools for themselves and provide teachers after their own choosing. Why should they request those who believe the Bible to pay the salaries of men who, not only do not believe the Bible themselves, but are determined to undermine the reasonable faith of the children? If the evidence proved the Book false, we would agree to reject it, but an investigation of all the data, which a critical science has produced, vindicates this Infallible Record.

At the Cincinnati meeting of The American Association for the Advancement of Science, 1923-24, a sparsely-attended session packed, for the most part with the ultra partisans of transformism, there was issued a dictatorial proclamation intended to be an authoritative edict which would silence for all time the protests of that great number who are neither superficial thinkers nor servile followers of a blatant pseudo-science. They could not, of course, refrain from hurling the usual rhetorical anathemas at Bryan, but these are amusing in their childishness and may be ignored.

The rash and intolerant decree which came from the throne-room, was as follows:

> "The evidences in favor of the evolution of man are sufficient to convince every scientist in the world."

This small group of fallible men, very unmindful of their own grievous limitations, forgot that scientific questions are not settled by authority, but exclusively, by means of irresistible evidence, which is certainly absent in this case. Moreover, the declaration is untrue. Many of the foremost palaeontologists and anthropologists of the day confess their complete ignorance as scientists, with respect to the origin of man.

Dr. Clark Wissler, Curator-in-Chief of the Anthropological Section of the American Museum of Natural History, New York, and an associate of Prof. Osborn, made this statement in an interview published in the New York American, April 2nd, 1918:

> "Man, like the horse or elephant, just happened anyhow. So far as has been discovered yet, there was always a man—some not so developed but still human beings in all their functions, much as we are today. Man came out of a blue sky as far as we have been able to delve back."

Prof. W. Branco, the great palaeontologist, Director of the Institute of Geology and Palaeontology of the University of Berlin, in his "Fossil

Man" said:

> "Palaeontology tells us nothing on the subject. It knows no ancestors of man."

Karl A. von Zittel, another well-known palaeontologist, reached the same conclusion. In "Grundzuge der Palaeontologie" he says:

> "Such material as this (the discovered remains of fossil men) throws no light upon the question of race and descent. All the human bones of determinable age that have come down to us from the European Diluvium, as well as all the skulls discovered in caves, are identified by their size, shape and capacity as belonging to Homo Sapiens (Modern Man) and are fine specimens of their kind. They do not by any means fill up the gap between man and the ape."

Joseph Le Conte repeats this refrain in his "Elements of Geology, Ch. VI. pg. 638. We read:

> "The earliest men yet found are in no sense connecting links between man and ape. They are distinctly human."

J. Reinke, the biologist of Kiel, writes in "Haeckel's Monism and Its Supporters":

> "We are merely having dust thrown in our eyes when we read in a widely circulated book ("Haeckel's Wettratsel") the following words:
> 'That man is immediately descended from apes, and more remotely from a long line of lower vertebrates, remains established as an indubitable historic fact, fraught with important consequences.'
> "It is absurd to speak of anything as a fact when experience lends it no support."

In another book, "Der Turmer," part 1, pg. 13,

the same author concludes:

> "The only statement consistent with her dignity that Science can make is to say that she knows nothing about the origin of man."

The illustrious Virchow writes in "The Liberty of Science," pg. 30:

> "We cannot teach, nor can we regard as one of the results of scientific research, the doctrine that man is descended from the ape or from any other animal."

Surely, in view of this great uncertainty and ignorance regarding the origin of the human body, it is extremely unethical to strive, as Osborn does, to impose the theory of man's bestial origin by the sheer weight of scientific authority and prestige. Those who respect their honor and dignity as scientists should refrain from dogmatizing on the undemonstrated animal origin of man, however much they may personally fancy their theory.

George O'Toole says: "The tone of scientific individuals and organizations threatens to become unduly imperious and intolerant, to forget limitations and to usurp the prerogative of infallibility." May we remind them of the slave who rode in the triumphal chariot of the Roman conqueror, to whisper ever and anon in his ear: "Hominem memento te!"—"Remember thou art a man?"

Was Darwin Right?

A reply to Sir Arthur Keith's Leeds, Eng., Address on "DARWIN"

By
ARTHUR I. BROWN
M. D. C. M., F. R. C. S. E.

Author of
Evolution and the Blood-Precipitation Test
Men, Monkeys and Missing Links
God's Creative Forethought
Evolution and the Bible
Etc.

Published by the
GLENDALE NEWS COMMERCIAL PRINTING CO.
137½ SOUTH BRAND BOULEVARD
GLENDALE, CALIFORNIA

DARWIN AND SIR ARTHUR KEITH

Judging by the amount of newspaper and magazine space devoted to it, quite a sensation has been caused by the recent presidential address of Sir Arthur Keith before the British Association for the Advancement of Science in August 1927 at Leeds, England. The subject of his speech was the present status of Darwin.

It had been commonly accepted even by the majority of evolutionary advocates that Darwin's sun was on the verge of eclipse. So many and so emphatic have been the declarations concerning the gross fallacies of Darwin's concept—declarations made by the most eminent scientists of the world—and so damaging and disheartening have been these adverse criticisms, that apparently Sir Arthur Keith considered the doctrine of transformism was in sore need of rehabilitation. What better means of rejuvenation could be imagined than to reinstate on his former pedestal of scientific eminence, Charles Darwin, the greatest proponent of a bestial ancestry for mankind?

Keith well knows that evolution stands or falls with what is called "Darwinism." Geo. Barry O'Toole gives this clear explanation of Darwinism as outlined by Darwin in 1859, in his book, "The Origin of Species:"

> "The naturalist bases the evolution of organic species upon the assumed spontaneous tendency of organisms to vary from their normal type in every possible direction. This spontaneous variability gives rise to slight variations, some of which are advantageous, others disadvantageous to the organism. The enormous fecundity of organisms multiplies them in excess of the available food supply, and more, accordingly,

are born than can possibly survive. In the ensuing competition or struggle for existence, individuals favorably modified survive and propagate their kind, those unfavorably modified perish without progeny. This process of elimination Darwin termed natural selection. Only individuals favored by it were privileged to propagate their kind, and thus it happened that these minute variations of a useful character were seized upon and perpetuated by the strong principle of inheritance. In this way these slight but useful modifications would tend gradually to accumulate from generation to generation in the direction favored by natural selection until, by the ensuing transmission of innumerable minor differences, verging in the same direction, a major difference would be produced. The end result would be a progressive divergence of posterity from the common ancestral type, whence they originally sprang, ending in a multiplicity of new forms or species, all differing to a greater or lesser extent from the primitive type."

That is, Darwin assumed what has never been proven, namely, the efficacy of natural selection. It rests on what has been disproved—the inheritance of the slight variations or fluctuations which are supposed to result in a gradual change of species. We have then the concepts of Variation, a Struggle for Existence owing to lack of sufficient food to support all animals born into the world, Natural Selection of certain characters, the transmission of which resulted in the survival of the fittest. In brief this constitutes Darwinism.

Keith says:

"Fifty-five years have come and gone since

—4—

Chas. Darwin wrote a history of man's descent. How does his work stand the test of time?.... An enormous body of new evidence has poured in upon us. We are now able to fill in many pages which Darwin had perforce to leave blank and we have found it necessary to alter details in his narrative, but the fundamentals of Darwin's outline of man's history remain unshaken. Nay, so strong has the position become that I am convinced it can never be shaken.

"Why do I say so confidently that Darwin's position has become impregnable? It is because of what has happened since his death in 1882. Since that time we have succeeded in tracing man by means of his fossil remains and by his stone implements backward in time to the very beginning of that period of earth's history to which the name of Pleistocene is given. We thus reach a point in history which is distant from us at least 200,000 years, perhaps three times that amount. Nay, we have gone further and traced him into the older and longer period which preceded the Pleistocene age. It was in strata laid down by a stream in Java during the latter part of the Pliocene period, that Dr. Eugene Dubois found ten years after Darwin's death the fossil remains of that remarkable representation of primitive humanity to which he gave the name of Pithecanthropus, or apeman."....

"If Darwin was right, then as we trace man backward in the scale of time he should become more bestial in form, nearer to the ape. That is what we have found. But if we regard Pithecanthropus with his small and simple yet human

—5—

brain as a fair representative of the man of the Pliocene period, then evolution must have proceeded very rapidly to bring higher races of mankind of today."

This language is that which we so constantly hear from the lips of evolutionists. When generalizing about their theory there is apparently no doubt whatever as to the fact of evolution, and it is only when we ask them to descend into details regarding the factors, and present some real proof of their position that we find out how woefully meagre the evidence is.

WHAT SCIENTISTS SAY

Before considering in detail some of the special points which Keith has made, we must examine the opinions of other eminent evolutionary authorities in regard to the present-day standing of Darwinism. Of course, natural selection and the transmission of acquired characters are the two basic concepts necessary for the successful operation of Darwin's idea, with inevitable transformation of many species. And here the evidence is so vast and so absolutely convincing and so diametrically opposed to Keith that one wonders by what process of mental juggling this eminent scientist is able to reach the conclusions which he so confidently proclaims.

Professor Wm. Bateson, the recently deceased biologist of England and certainly one of the greatest authorities of the past century, in his presidential address to the British Association in 1915, made this momentous statement:

"Through the last 50 years this theme of natural selection of favored races has been developed and expounded in writings innumerable. Favored races certainly can replace others. The argument is sound but we are

—6—

doubtful of its value. For us that debate stands adjourned. We go to Darwin for his incomparable collection of facts. We would vain emulate his scholarship, his width, and his power of expression, but **to us he speaks no more with philosophical authority.** We read his scheme of evolution as we would those of Lucretius or Lamarck, delighting in their simplicity and their courage."

And again Bateson, speaking before the American Association, said:

"While 40 years ago the Darwinian theory was accepted without question; today scientists have come to a point where they are unable to offer any explanation for the genesis of species. **There is no evidence of any one species acquiring new factors.** But there are plenty of examples of species losing factors. Species lose things but do not add to their possessions. Variations of many kinds we daily witness, but **no origin of species.**"

Geo. Barry O'Toole in "The Case Against Evolution" page 12, writes:

"William Bateson warns those who persist in their credulity with reference to the Darwinian account of organic teleology, that they will be wise henceforth to base this faith frankly on the impregnable rock of superstition and to abstain from direct appeals to natural fact. This admission forms the conclusion of a scathing criticism of what he styles the "Fustian of Victorian Philosophy."

In his Toronto address on December 28, 1921, Bateson said:

"But that particular and essential bit of the

—7—

theory of evolution which is concerned with the original nature of species remains utterly mysterious. We no longer feel as we used to do, that the process of variation now contemporaneously occurring is the beginning of a work which needs merely the element of time for its completion; for even time cannot complete that which has not yet begun. The conclusion on which we were brought up that species are a product of the summation of variations, ignored the chief attribute of species first pointed out by John Ray, that the product of their crosses is frequently sterile in greater or less degree.

In Science, January 20, 1926, Bateson writes:

"The production of an indubitably sterile hybrid from completely fertile parents which has arisen under critical observation is the event for which we wait. Until this event is witnessed or known of, evolution is incomplete in a vital respect. From time to time such an observation is published, but none has yet survived criticism."

Bateson also writes in the same issue of Science:

"Analysis has revealed hosts of transferable characters. Their combinations suffice to supply in abundance, series of types which might pass for new species, and certainly would be so classed if they were met with in nature. Yet critically tested, we find that they are not distinct species and we have no reason to suppose any accumulation of characters of the same order would culminate in the production of distinct species. Specific difference therefore must be regarded as probably attaching to the base upon which these transferables are im-

—8—

planted, of which we know absolutely nothing at all. **Nothing that we have witnessed in the contemporary world can colorably be interpreted as providing the sort of evidence required.**"

In 1922, speaking at the British meeting, he said:

"It is impossible for scientists to agree with Darwin's theory of the origin of species. No explanation whatever has been offered for the fact that **after 40 years no evidence has been discovered to verify his genesis of species.**"

Professor Bateson's last writing on evolution is found in the 13th edition of the Encyclopedia Britannica in his article on Mendelism, in which he gives his considered and mature judgment in regard to the present status of evolution.

In this essay Bateson says that a great stimulus was imparted to the study of heredity and variation by the rediscovery of Mendel's paper.

"Current beliefs among naturalists were at once found to be largely incorrect. The assumed appearance of variableness is largely illusory. Of the occurrence of the genetic change which might be likely to lead to the production of new species, none has been found."

His startling conclusion is that:

"The immediate consequence has been that the development of the evolutionary theory has been tacitly suspended or postponed."

Professor W. B. Scott, Professor of Geology and Paleontology in Princeton University, in his book "The Theory of Evolution," on page 20, writes:

"Darwin's pet theory, that of natural selection, was not so fortunate....There has always been a large body of opinion which rejected it as vague, inadequate and unsatisfactory, and there have been many attempts to submit or substitute some more convincing explanation for it."

He further says:

Personally, I have never been satisfied that Darwin's theory is the rightful one; to one who approaches the problem from the study of fossils, the doctrine of natural selection does not appear to offer an adequate explanation of the observed facts. The doctrine, in its application to concrete cases, is vague, elastic, unconvincing and seems to leave the whole process to chance. On the other hand, if Darwin's hypothesis be rejected, there is, it must be frankly admitted, no satisfactory alternative to take its place."

Dr. D. H. Scott, the eminent British botanist, addressing the 1921 meeting of the British Association, said:

"For the moment at all events, the Darwinian period is past; we can no longer enjoy the comfortable assurance which once satisfied so many of us, that the main problem has been solved—all is again in the melting pot. But now, in fact, a new generation has grown up that knows not Darwin. Is even then evolution not a scientifically ascertained fact? **No! We must hold it as an act of faith because there is no alternative.**

Geo. Barry O'Toole, in his book "The Case Against Evolution," page 10, writes of Darwin:

"His hypothesis leaves the origin of variations an unsolved mystery...Darwin erred no less with respect to the spontaneity, than with respect to

—10—

the inheritability and summation, of his "slight variations." Spencer refused to see any value whatever in Darwin's principle of natural selection, while other Neo-Lamarckians, less extreme, were content to relegate it to the status of a subordinate factor in evolution....**It is safe to say that no modern biologist attaches very much importance to natural selection.** Natural selection making the organism a product of the concurrence of blind force unguided by Divine intelligence, a mere fortuitous result, and not the realization of purpose, has furnished the agnostic with a miserable pretext for omitting God from his attempted explanation of the universe....Its scientific insolvencies have become so painfully apparent that **biologists have lost all confidence in its power to solve the problem** of organic origins."

On page 29, O'Toole writes:

"It is almost pitiful to hear the die-hards of Darwinism bolstering up a lost cause with the wretched quibble that though natural selection has been discredited as an explanation of the differentiation of species, Darwinism "in its essentials" survives intact, for if there is any feature which, beyond all else deserves to be called an essential of Darwin's system, surely it is natural selection. For Darwin it was "the most important" agency of transformation. Apart from his hypothesis of the summation through inheritance of slight variations, now completely demolished by the new science of genetics, it represented his sole contribution to the philosophy of transformism. It alone distinguishes Darwinism from Lamarckism, its pro-

—11—

totype—....**Darwinism is dead, and no grief of mourners can resuscitate the corpse."**

Professor L. T. More, Physicist of Cincinnatti University in "The Dogma of Evolution" writes a strong section on Darwinism. On page 194 he says:

"Unfortunately for Darwin's future reputation, his life was spent on the problem of evolution which is deductive by nature....It is absurd to expect that many facts will not always be irreconcilable with any theory of evolution and, today, **every one of his arguments is contradicted by facts."**

More says also:

"Four years after the publication of the "Origin of Species," Darwin wrote Bentham that: 'The belief in natural selection must at present be grounded entirely on general considerations. When we descend to details we **can prove that no species has changed; nor can we prove that the supposed changes are beneficial, which is the ground work of the theory."**

On page 199:

"The failure of natural selection is largely due to its foundation of false philosophy."

On page 215:

"Even from a scientific aspect, Darwin's work to establish natural selection is rapidly crumbling on its biological side."

On page 221:

"New varieties and races created by artificial selection revert to the original type as soon as they are left to their own devices....There are fewer features in common between natural and artificial selection than the Darwinian supposed."

—12—

On page 227:

"Darwin's attention was called to the fact that if only a few individuals possessed advantageous variation, the effect of chance mating would prevent its continuance since there would be little probability of these few individuals mating together, In the sixth edition, **Darwin admits the justice of this criticism, and in doing so, he absolutely abandons his own theory of natural selection.**"

On page 231:

"Even the basic principle itself, the struggle for existence as the predominating factor in organic life, is now attacked on all sides...Sexual selection is at the present time harshly criticized and even abandoned by most naturalists."

On page 237:

"Professor Bateson carefully knocks down every prop to natural selection, to the inheritance of acquired traits, and to evolution in general; then he concludes by asking us to apply the doctrine of evolution to the thoughts and actions of man because he still has faith in evolution and some day biologists may find its solution. Delage offers enough objections to evolution by natural selection to kill even the most desirable theory."

Henry Fairfield Osborn, President of the American Museum of Natural History and one of the foremost evolutionists of the day, in speaking before the British Association meeting at Oxford, said:

"We may as well face the facts, that the cause of the origin of species may never be known. Research seems to be fatal to the speculations of Lamarck and Darwin. If living today,

—13—

Darwin would be the foremost in modifying his theory. **Darwin was brave but wrong."**

Richard Swann Lull, Professor of Vertebrate Paleontology in Yale University, writing in "Organic Evolution," 1924, on page 101, says:

"Not all authorities accept natural selection **as an important** factor....Many believe that natural selection has nothing to do with species forming....Still another Darwinian factor is sexual selection, the means whereby Darwin sought to explain the existence of what are known as the secondary sexual characters amongst animals....As we shall see, this is the most doubtful factor of all those advocated by Darwin and **is only held because nothing has been offered in its place."**

And to lessen the effect of his criticism, Lull, using the usual confident language, says:

"But it must be borne in mind that however much Darwin may be assailed, the word refers only to certain of these causal factors, leaving the citadel of the evolutionary doctrine as impregnable as ever."

Dr. E. Dennert, the well-known German authority, in his convincing work "At the Deathbed of Darwinism" deals many scathing blows at this doctrine, and gives the opinions of many scientists. He presents the decidedly adverse judgment of many eminent authorities who totally rejected Darwinism, and mentions among other scientists of 25 years ago: Wigand, Hans Driesch, O. Hannan, Haacke, and Wilser, who said at the convention of Naturalists in 1897:

"No one who has committed himself to Darwinism can longer be ranked as a naturalist."

He refers to Julius von Sachs, the most gifted and

—14—

brilliant botanist of the last century, as bitterly opposed to Darwin, also Dr. Carl Camille Schneider, Assistant at the Zoological Institute of the University of Vienna; Dr. Goatte, the Strassburg biologist; the botanists, Professor Korschinsky and Professor Haberlandt; also some of the most eminent paleontologists such as Professor Steinman, who summarizes his conclusions as follows:

1. "**The family and transition forms demanded from palaeontology by Darwinism for its family-trees, constructed not empirically but a priori, are nowhere to be found among the abundant materials which palaeontological investigations has already produced.**"

2. "The results of the investigation do not correspond with the family groups drawn up according to the so-called "biogenetic principle," which principle has in fact led men of science into false paths.

3. "At best, the biogenetic principle has a limited validity, (we add that later it will undoubtedly follow Darwinism and its family trees into the lumber-room).

4. "**The results of paleontology, in so far, for instance, as they testify to the sudden disappearance of the saurians and the advent of mammals, everywhere contradict the Darwinian principle of the survival of the fittest in the struggle for existence.**

5. "The time has long passed when the Darwinian explanations were regarded with naive confidence as the alpha and omega of the doctrine of Descent.

6. "Only the principle of Descent is universally recognized; the 'how' of it, its

—15—

causes, are today entirely a matter of dispute."

Dennert gives some strong evidence from Professor Eimer, Professor of Zoology, Tuebingen, proving the untenableness of Darwin's position. Dennert says:

"Darwinism has been rejected, not on account of a lack of research, but on account of abundance of research, which proved its absolute insufficiency....It is an incontrovertible fact that the hereditary transmission of acquired characters has in no way been proved....If acquired characters are not transmitted by heredity, Darwinism is an impossibility....Experience has made it certain that Darwinism has everywhere failed."

He quotes Grottewitz on p. 119:

"There is no doubt that a number of Darwinian views which are still prevalent today, have sunk to the level of untenable myths.... The Darwinian doctrines are incapable of being strictly and irrefutably demonstrated...Darwin's theory of chance is nothing more than a myth. The origin of one species from another, the conservation of the useful forms, the existence of countless intermediary links are all assumptions, which could never be supported by concrete cases found in actual experience."

Professor Fleischman of Erlangen, the famous Zoologist, is highly praised by Professor W. B. Scott of Princeton. In his book "Die Descendenz Theorie," he writes:

"After long and careful investigation I have come to the conclusion that the doctrine of Descent has not been substantiated. I go even farther and maintain that the discussion of the

—16—

question does not belong to the field of the exact sciences of zoology and botany....Research must show that living organisms actually **have** overstepped the bounds dividing their species, and not merely that they conceivably **may** have done so....The evolution of the vertebrates from the fish is a wholly gratuitous assumption devoid of any foundation in fact."

J. Arthur Thomson, Professor of Natural History in the University of Aberdeen, writing in "Outline of Science," vol, 2, page 365, on "How Darwinism Stands Today," says:

"We are more keenly aware than in Darwin's day of our ignorance as to the origin and affiliation of the greater classes....It would be a sorry business if Darwinism stood today as it was left by Darwin....It would be a terrible contradiction in terms if an evolutionary theory did not itself evolve!....Our frankness in admitting difficulties and relative ignorance in regard to the variations and selections that lead from some dinosaurs to birds, cannot be used by any fair-minded inquirer as an argument against the idea of evolution, for how else could birds have arisen?"

On page 371, he writes:

"Since Darwin's time evidence has accumulated which shows that variations are more definite than used to be supposed."

This is rather an unfortunate admission because definiteness in variation does not lend itself to support the theory of chance evolution. Again on page 371, he says:

"One of the great changes that has come about since Darwin's day is a recognition of the

—17—

frequency of discontinuous variations by which we mean sudden novelties, which are not connected with the type of species by intermediate gradations."

Of course Darwin's theory was that of small, gradual, intermediate gradation. This "great change" mentioned by Thomson is surely and fatally opposed to Darwinism. On page 377, we read:

"We must join with Darwin in saying 'Our ignorance of the laws of variation is profound.'"

In his conclusion, page 388, he states:

"It must be said that while the main ideas remain valid, there has been development all along the line. Darwinism has evolved as every sound theory should.

"There is at present among zoologists a wide spread agreement with Sir Ray Lankester's pronouncement that one of the notable advances since Darwin's day has been getting rid of the Lamarckian theory of the transmission of individually acquired characters, or imprinted bodily modifications...The facts are not at present in favor of the Lamarckian view."

With great naivete he remarks:

"We may perhaps look for an evolution of Lamarckism as well as of Darwinism....One of the changes since Darwin's day is the recognition that variations are often very definite.... Another change from Darwinism, is the Mendelian idea of unit characters which behave like entities in inheritance. They are handed on with a strong measure of intactness to a certain proportion of the offspring. Since Darwin's day there have been in a few cases definite proofs of natural selection at work....Darwinism has changed and is changing, but it is not crumbling away. It is evolving progressively."

It is amusing to see how great men of intelligence persist in holding to a pet theory in spite of the most obvious and conclusive facts in opposition to it. Thomson admits that the transmission of acquired characters is disproved by scientific investigations, making impossible any Darwinian mode of evolution, and yet, in spite of this evident fact, he concludes that "Darwinism stands today more firmly than ever."

It would seem to be beyond discussion that all the concepts of Darwin have ignominiously been set aside and trampled under foot by a skeptical science. If "it has changed and is changing," why in the name of uncommon sense is it not "crumbling away?"

Dr. Caullery, writing in Science, April 21, 1916, uses these words:

"Since the time of Darwin, Natural Selection has remained purely a speculative idea."

John Burroughs, one of America's leading naturalists said, in Atlantic Monthly, August 1920:

"Darwin has been shorn of his selection theory as completely as Samson was shorn of his locks."

J. T. Cummings quoted British scientists in Nature, March 3, 1923, saying:

"I venture to say that few who have made a special and practical study of evolution, and are well acquainted with recent progress in that study, have much faith in natural selection."

Writing on paleontology in the Encyclopedia Britannica, p. 520, Osborn says:

"The net result of observation is not favorable to the essentially Darwinian view that the adaptive arises out of the fortuitous by selection, but is rather favorable to the hypothesis of the existence of some quite unknown intrinsic law of life, which we are at present totally unable to comprehend or even perceive."

Professor Vernon Kellogg of Stanford University writing in "Darwinism—Today," p. 5, says:

"The fair truth is that the Darwinin selection theories considered with regard to their claimed capacity to be an independently mechanical explanation of descent, stand today seriously discredited in the biological world. On the other hand it is also fair to say that no replacing hypothesis or theory of species forming has been offered by the opponents of selection, which has met with any general or even considerable acceptance by naturalists."

KEITH SAYS

To return to Keith, he continues:

"Why do I say so confidently that Darwinism has become impregnable?"

Now this is precisely what we would like to know and we shall expect convincing evidence warranting the sublime faith of this ardent evolutionary advocate before we consider the case proven.

Then follows the proof: The first item seems to be certain alleged fossil remains of man which have been unearthed since Darwin's day.

Keith says:

"It is because of what has happened since his death in 1882. Since then we have succeeded in tracing man by means of his fossil remains and by his stone implements backward in time to the very beginning of that period of the earth's history to which the name Pleistocene is given....distant from us at least 200,000 years, perhaps three times that amount. Nay, we have gone further....and have traced him into the Pliocene....Dr. Eugene Du Bois found, ten years after Darwin's death, the fossil remains of that remarkable representative of primitive humanity, a pithecanthropus or ape-man....If Darwin was right, then as we trace man backward in the scale of time he should become more bestial in form, nearer to the ape. That is what we have found."

Then he speaks of the "small and simple, yet human brain" of Pithecanthropus, and affirms that "evolution must have proceeded at an unexpectedly rapid rate to culminate today in the higher races of mankind."

Certainly this latter observation of Keith's is the wisest in the whole address. In fact, progress must have been miraculously swift and gigantic.

Keith outlines Darwin's method of proof under three heads:

1. "He gathered historical documents from the body and behaviour of man and compared them with the observations made on the body and behaviour of every animal which showed the least resemblance to man." This, of course, is the old comparative anatomy argument.

2. "He studied all that was known in his day of man's embryological history."

3. "He took into consideration the manner in which the living tissues of man react to disease, to drugs, to environment." This of course is just another form of the comparative anatomy argument.

"By a logical analysis of his facts, Darwin reconstructed and wrote a history of man."

These three lines of Darwin's investigation as mentioned by Keith are supplemented by what he calls "an enormous body of new evidence." As far as one can gather from the address, this new evidence consists, first, of fossil remains. In fact, Keith says that such evidence is "definite and irrefutable." These fossil remains are two, Pithecanthropus and the Piltdown man. The second line of new evidence, according to the speaker, is that from examination of blood based on the experiments of Nuttall of Cambridge University. Third, the similarity between the brains of man and anthropoid apes. Fourth, Vestigial structures in the human body.

Keith goes on to say: "We have to seek out the biological processes and controlling influences which have shaped the evolutionary history of man and ape. The evolution of new styles of man or of ape is one thing, and the evolution of new types of motor cars is another, yet for the purpose of **clear** thinking it will repay us to use the one example to illustrate the other. In the evolution of motor vehicles, Darwin's law of selection has prevailed....The **public** has selected its favorite types of cars but it has had no direct authority in designing and producing modifications and improvements."

Then he says that in order to understand the machinery underlying evolution,—"we must enter the 'factories' where the evolutionary changes are being produced, that is, we must examine the ovum as it is formed into an embryo, the embryo changing into a foetus, and the foetus into a babe." After birth he asks us to note "infancy passing to childhood, childhood into adolescence, adolescence into maturity, and maturity into old age."

He then deals with the potent and mysterious substances called hormones, which he says "were not dreamed of in Darwin's time, when also experimental

—22—

embryology was scarcely born." He pictures the body of a growing child as an immense society made up of "myriads of microscopic living units, ever increasing in numbers. One of the ways—probably the oldest and most important way—in which the activities of the communities of the body are coordinated and regulated is by the postal system discovered by Starling, wherein the missives are hormones—chemical substances in ultra-microscopic amounts, dispatched from one community to another in the circulating blood. Clearly a discovery of this ancient and intricate system opens up fresh vistas to the student of man's evolution. How Darwin would have welcomed this discovery."

In fairness to the lecturer, his closing paragraph ought to be given:

"What is man's origin? Was Darwin right when he said that man, under the action of biological forces which can be observed and measured has been raised from a place among anthropoid apes to that which he now occupies? The answer is Yes! And in rendering this verdict I speak but as a foreman of the jury—a jury which has been empaneled from men who have devoted a lifetime to weighing the evidence. To the best of my ability, I have avoided, in laying before you the evidence on which our verdict was found, the roll of special pleader, being content to follow Darwin's own example—Let the truth speak for itself."

In the early part of his address, Keith says that in the city of Leeds "was fired the first verbal shot of that long and bitter strife which ended in the overthrow of those who defended the Biblical account of man's creation and in a victory for Darwin." The implication throughout Keith's address is that the Biblical account is absolutely wrong and this is the reason why every where athiests and unbelievers are snatching at this speech like a hungry dog at a bone.

These constitute all the arguments brought forward by Keith to prove his case and each of these will now be considered specifically.

COMPARATIVE ANATOMY

Does Comparative Anatomy or the resemblances existing between animals and man prove evolution of the one into the other? These similarities are obvious and admitted by all, but it is well to remember this cardinal fact that "similarity in structure is no proof of genetic or blood relationship." The fact that animals have practically the same number of bones and muscles as man, and similar organs and tissues in order to perform the same functions, is certainly no proof that man is descended from a bestial ancestry. The Creationists occupy a firm and impregnable position. God, the Creator, conceived and created the animal, providing the animal with a bodily structure similar in its form and makeup to that of man. For instance, the Creator decided that animals should breathe air—man likewise. Therefore there is no conceivable reason why both should not be given lungs. Eating similar food, they would require similar stomachs and digestive apparatus; performing the functions of standing, walking, running, they would require the same number of bones and muscles. Similarity in structure proves nothing more than a common basic plan of architecture.

This plan is seen everywhere today. When man builds a shack on the desert, a bungalow, a two storied house, or a large apartment, the same basic plan is adopted. Is there any reason why the Divine Architect should not do the same thing in His creative work? God does but one kind of work, the best possible, and if he gave animals less or more structures than man, the

—24—

finished product would not be absolutely perfect, which would be impossible for an Omniscient Creator. This is all that Comparative Anatomy proves.

Osborn confesses the weakness of this argument in the Encyclopedia Britannica, Vol. 20, p. 580:

"From comparative anatomy alone, it is possible to arrange a series of living forms which, although structurally a convincing array, because **placed** in a graduating series, may be, nevertheless, in an order inverse to that of the actual historical succession."

Professor D'Arcy Thompson in his book "On Growth and Form," writing on this argument from homologies or resemblances, says:

"But this great generalization is apt, in my opinion, to carry us too far. It will be safe and sure, and helpful, and illuminating, when we apply it to such complex entities—resultants of the combination and permutation of many variable characters, as a horse, a lion, or an eagle; but (to my mind) it has a very different look and a far less firm foundation, when we attempt to extend it to minute organisms whose specific characters are few and simple, when regarded from the point of view of physical and mathematical description and analysis, and whose form is referable, or (to say the least of it) is very largely referable to the direct and immediate action of a particular physical force.

"Certain resemblances are the result of similar forces playing on similar material; differences happen when dissimilar forces impinge on different material. The zoologist must begin with mathematics."

Professor Otto, writing of Professor Kremer's book,

"The Natural History of Plants," disposes of the first argument in favor of the theory of Descent, the homology of individual organisms, by explaining that:

"Homology is due to the similarity of function in the different organisms....Homology of organisms is no proof of their hereditary affiliation."

Professor St. Geo. Mivart says in his book, "Lessons in Nature:"

"Experience more and more convinces me that the number of similarities which have arisen independently is prodigious, as well as that very great caution is needed in endeavoring to discriminate between likenesses etc....."

Professor O'Toole effectively demolishes the argument from homology in "The Case Against Evolution." He says:

"To suppose that inheritance alone can account for structural resemblances is unwarranted assumption....The mechanists have succeeded in extracting from the facts, not what the facts themselves proclaim, but what preexisted in their own highly cultured imaginations, so well stocked with cogs, cranks, ball bearings, and other aesthetic imagery, emanating from polytechnic schools and factories...In these universal properties of living matter, therefore, we have a common basis for general structural and organizational laws, quite adequate to account for both the homologies and analyses of living matter."

On page 63, he writes:

"But, when it be upon, or beneath the surface, similitude of any kind suffices to establish our contention that inheritance is not the only

—26—

similifying influence present in organisms, and that resemblance is perfectly compatible with independence of ancestry.

He sums up his argument by saying:

> "The evolutionary argument from homology is defective in three important respects:
>
> (1) In its lack of experimental confirmation; (2) In its incomplete enumeration of the disjunctive possibilities; (3) In its inability to construct a scheme of transmutation that synthesizes inheritance and variation in a logically coherent and factually substantiated formula."

We shall now notice Darwin's argument from embryology. The evolutionist seeks to explain from the study of the human embryo that he discovers in the early stages of development many animal parts which are subsequently changed or discarded as the human characters become dominant. Also the "recapitulation theory" is used to prove that in our individual development before birth we recapitulate or repeat the history of the race. It is alleged that the human body passes through various changes of species similar to those characterizing the history of the race during past milleniums. What standing among scientists has this theory?

Professor W. B. Scott of Princeton says in "Readings in Evolution" p. 173:

> "Thirty years ago the recapitulation theory was well nigh universally accepted....Haeckel called this theory the "fundamental biogenetic law," and upon it he established his whole "History of Creation." Nowadays, this "fundamental law" is very seriously questioned and by some high authorities is altogether denied."

—27—

Professor Thos. H. Morgan of Columbia University, writing in "Evolution and Adaptation," p. 83, states:

"It seems to me that the idea that ancestral stages have been pushed back into the embryo, and that the embryo recapitulates in part these ancestral adult stages, is in principle false."

The Scientific American, Feb. 1921, p. 121, quoting Professor A. Weber of the University of Geneva, says:

"The critical comments of such embryologists as O. Hertwig, Keibel, Vialleton, indeed, have practically torn to shreds the aforesaid fundamental biogenetic law. Its almost unanimous abandonment has left considerably at a loss those investigators who sought in the structure of organisms the key to their remote origin or to their relationshps."

P. C. Mitchell in his article "Evolution" in the Encyclopedia Britannica says:

"The most striking general change has been against seeing in the fact of ontogeny (embryonic development) any direct evidence as to philogeny (ancestral history)."

Geo. McCready Price in "The Phantom of Organic Evolution," quotes Percy Davidson as follows:

"From these authoritative statements it appears that the facts of embryonic resemblances fail to support recapitulation in all three of its main implications."

Price also quotes Geoffrey Smith, who writes in "Primitive Animals:"

"When we attempt to go behind philogeny and discover their origin and interrelationships, we leave the firm ground altogether and wander in a slippery and nebulous region of speculation....It is true that certain hypotheses of a plausible character have been suggested which have satisfied uncritical minds, and which we often hear advanced as a part of ascertained science and accepted in an otiose spirit....But what is there of reality in these speculations? They rest not on any objective evidence but on the tendency of the mind to pass from the apparently simple to the manifestly complex, and to regard the former as primitive and ancestral, and the latter as secondary and derivative."

Professor Karl Vogt, Geneva writes:
"This law which I long held as well founded, is absolutely and radically false."

Professor Adam Sedgwick, the very eminent English Embryologist, in his book "Darwinism and Modern Science," p. 174, says:
"But as Huxley has shown and as the whole course of paleontological investigation has demonstrated, no such statement can be made (that this law of recapitulation is true.) The extinct forms of life are very similar to those now existing, and there is nothing especially embryonic about them. So that the facts as we know them, lend no support to the theory (of recapitulation)."

And, on page 176, he writes:
"After fifty years of research and close examination of the facts of embryology, the recapitulation theory is still without satisfactory proof."

Kellogg, in "Darwinism To Day," pp. 18, 21, says:
"The proof that man is descended from a

fish because he had gill slits at one period in his individual development, is not of the sort to rely on too confidently. The recapitulation theory of Fritz Muller and Haeckel is chiefly conspicuous now as a skeleton on which to hang innumerable exceptions."

"The recapitulation theory is mostly wrong and what is right in it is mostly so covered up by the wrong part that few biologists longer have any confidence in discovering the right." Wasmann, in "Modern Biology" says:

"Do the facts warrant the assertion that the individual development of every creature is in variable and the recapitulation of the history of the race? No, they do not, for the exceptions to this rule are far more numerous than the instances of it.' (p. 449)

And even Keith himself in "The Human Body," p. 95, has to admit:

"Now that the appearances of the embryo at all stages are known, the general feeling is one of disappointment; the human embryo at no stage is anthropoid in its appearance."

Are we not justified, in the light of these author itive judgments, in saying that the study of the embryo gives no support whatever to the evolutionary hy pothesis?

BLOOD TEST

Another argument of Keith's as outlined above is from the examination of blood. Professor Nuttall con ducted 16,000 experiments, so it is stated, in 1904; this evidence is 24 years of age and rather antiquated to be brought forward as recent evidence.

Keith says:

"He found the blood of man and that of the

great anthropoid apes gave almost the same reaction. Bacteriologists find that the living anthropoid body possesses almost the same susceptiveness to infections and manifest the same reactions as does the body of man."

Certainly to anyone who knows the results of these tests it would appear very difficult to derive much evolutionary comfort from them. Some of the results are not only exceedingly peculiar but manifestly absurd. As a matter of fact, in the experiments, the blood is allowed to clot, a process which removes not only the life principle but also all the solid elements. All that is left is the watery serum which forms the basis of the blood, and might, without giving any support to evolution, be similar in both man and animals.

In the list of results that are given, table "A" indicates that old world monkeys are eight points removed from man, while new world monkeys are 22 points distant. But table "B" shows O.W.M. 35 points away from man and anthropoids, a discrepancy of 27 degrees between the two tables.

But table "C" proves O.W.M., man, and anthropoids to be practically identical, while table "D," to add to our confusion, gives 13 points between O.W.M. and man and 27 points between man and anthropoids. But table "E," to make matters worse, suggests that man is a real ape! Also, he seems to be a monkey—O.W.M. species. We would like to know really what man is anyway? Table "C" reveals the fact the O.W.M. and N.W.M. are 42 points apart, but in table "D" an impassable gulf of 64 points yawns between.

Table "A" does not permit the marmoset and O.W.M. to come closer together than 42 points, but table "D" increases the distance to 64.

In table "D," anti-sheep serum was used on horses and other animals. According to one test, horses and

—31—

sheep are 84 degrees removed. In this same table where wild pig serum was used against horses and sheep, the two latter animals are close brothers, separated by only three points.

In table "E," pig and horse seem to be about the same kind of animal, 20 and 16 respectively, but in the next method, a tremendous chasm of 74 points separates them. In the one, sheep and dog are 93 points apart, while in the other they are identical.

Nuttall also gives the results of quantitative tests in which he measured the amount of precipitin as deposit produced by the various bloods tested. Some of the results are so exceedingly peculiar that it is difficult to see how any conclusions of value can be drawn.

In the first test, jackall, otter, ox, sheep, and Tibetan bear show a definite relation to man. In the second and third tests, one species of baboon is as closely related to man, and a short tailed O.W.M. more closely related than the ape.

In another test, in which the actual proportion of deposit is given very exactly in decimals, horse, sheep, and baboon are grouped together with .004; and the whalebone whale, one species of baboon, the tiger, the African anthropoid and man, are the same, .003.

In the second test, man, the civet cat, the tenrec, a little mammal of Madagascar, are all on the same level, .001. Certainly, while not noble, our forbears are numerous! Even Professor W. B. Scott, friendly as he is to the evidence of evolution, has to admit: "It could hardly be maintained that an ostrich and a parrot are more nearly alike than a wolf and a hyena, and yet that would be the inference from blood tests."

In his Berlin "Discussion of Evolution," Eric Wasmann most emphatically refutes a number of these confident claims for blood and he writes of these same 16,000 experiments of Nuttall:

"We are not justified in regarding a chemical and physiological resemblance as constituting a blood relationship in the sense of having a common origin. Let us assume that there is a blood resemblance between the blood of apes and that of man. This would prove that the same kind of likeness existed in the blood of man and apes, as in their skeletons and other organs, but similarity does not imply blood relation, such as exists between cousins and kinsfolk....And the blood reaction points to a close relation between creatures that are morphologically far apart. It would seem that we cannot make much of evidence derived from similarity of blood if comparative morphology arrives at different results. More recent investigators, Uhlenhuth, and Friedenthal, attempt to throw a doubt on the alleged actual existence of similarity between human blood and that of higher apes, and this circumstance renders untenable all the conclusions based on the similarity, viz., that man is closely related to the higher apes, or is even an ape himself."

Even Professor Nuttall seems to realize the difficulties inherent in his experiments because he writes:

"In viw of the crudity of our methods, it is not surprising that certain discrepancies may be encountered in the course of investigations conducted bv biological methods."

In his book he devotes 15 pages to "Sources of Error," showing how great is the risk of mistakes, which must invalidate every conclusion. Certainly this blood argument is one of the weakest brought forward by the believer in evolution.

—33—

VESTIGIAL ORGANS

Next we consider the argument from vestigial organs.

Keith says:

"We find the same vestigial structures—the same "evolutionary postmarks—in the body of man and anthropoid."

Vestigial remains are tissues or organs found in the human body for which there is no known use and which are alleged to be remnants or vestiges of a pre-human existence. Since mankind has attained the present high point of development, these vestiges have shrunken and atrophied and are now useless incumbrances according to this view. The claim is one of the most grotesque in all the realm of evolutionary imaginings.

Dr. P. C. Mitchell in Encyclopedia Britannica, vol. 20, p. 33, writes:

"It is almost impossible to prove that any structure, however rudimentary, is useless, and if it is in the slightest degree useful, there is no reason why, on the hypothesis of direct creation, it should not have been created."

Even Keith himself, writing in "Nature" a few months ago, eliminated the appendix from the list of vestigial organs and made this significant remark:

"As our knowledge increases the vestigial organs decrease."

MISSING LINKS

Keith attaches great importance to two specimens of alleged 'missing links,' as providing irrefutabe evidence for evolution. One cannot help but admire Keith's

—34—

courage in bringing forward these two grotesque and long since exploded bits of evidence.

Of the first, Pithecanthropus Erectus or the Java apeman, R. R. Marrett writes in "Anthropology:"

"By itself stands the so called Pithecanthropus (ape man) of Java, a regular missing link....It must remain, however, highly doubtful whether this is a proto human being or merely an ape of a type related to the gibbon. This, if an ape, has an enormous brain; if a man, he must have verged on what we would consider idiocy.... (p. 76)

Prof. E. Metchnikoff, late Head of the Pasteur Institute, at Paris, says, in "Nature of Man," p. 49:

"The facts about this creature are meagre and have been interpreted differently."

Prof. E. D. Cope, in "Primary Factors of Organic Evolution," is doubtful....as to all the bones belonging to one and the same skeleton, when he says:

"The tooth was found close to the skull and belongs **probably** to the same individual as the latter, while the reference to the femur is more uncertain as it was found some fifty feet distant. (p. 169).

Prof. Wm. Hertwig, in his book, "Zoology," declares:

"The opinion that is most probably correct is that the fragments belonged to an anthropo morphic ape of extraordinary rize, and an enor mous cranial capacity with a relatively large brain."

E. Wasmann, in "Modern Biology and the Theory of Evolution," gives his opinion as follows:

"It is nothing short of an outrage upon truth,

—35—

to represent scanty remains, the origin of which is so uncertain as that of the pithecanthropus, as absolute proof of the descent of man from beasts, in order thus to deceive the general public."

Adverse criticisms similar to the above, abound in the literature, but the opinion which probably carries the most weight, is that of Prof. Rudolph Virchow, for thirty years, President of the Berlin Anthropological Society, and surely one of the world's greatest authorities, not second to Sir Arthur Keith, in any respect.

Wasmann, in "Modern Biology," p. 465, writes that

"Virchow uttered a very courteous but crushing criticism upon the speaker's remarks, and showed it was by no means certain that the remains had all formed part of the same individual and that it was still less possible to decide whether that individual was a man or an ape."

In December of the same year, Virchow, having further examined the skull, said that he had come to the clear conclusion that the skull had not belonged to a man, but that it showed greatest similarity to the skull of a hylobates (gibbon). According to all the rules of classification, he considered the being an animal, and indeed an ape. He had compared the original drawing made by Dr. Dubois, with the skull of a hylo bates, and there was as great similarity as one could expect between two individuals of the same species. As to the teeth, they appeared much more ape-like than human, In regard to the thigh bone, he said, that in spite of its similarity to that of man, there was so much agreement with that of a gibbon, that he saw no diffi culty in its having belonged to a large-size hylobates (gibbon).

Dr. J. H. F. Kohlbrugge, in "Die Morphologie Abstamung des Menchen," says

"....This opinion compared with others that have been cited, shows that we have not here to deal merely with comparisons with one, two, or three unknown forms, but that the number of the great unknown grows so large that our actual knowledge becomes a small point upon which a hypothetical pyramid is built with its basis in the air. The great antiquity ascribed to Pithecanthropus appears to be altogether doubtful. Nothing compels us to conclude that the thigh bone and the skull belong to one another."

What is the reputation of the second fossil proof (?) which Keith mentions? Is he justified in saying that the Piltdown Man, otherwise known as Eoanthropus Dawsoni, constitutes a real link in man's descent from animals?"

When this specimen was first found, Prof. Keith, curator of the Museum of the Royal College of Surgeons, London, Eng., did not think very highly of it, and demonstrated that the brain capacity of the Piltdown skull, was not 1070 c.c., the very convenient evidential size given it by its finders, in their effort to see an intermediary form between man and ape, but nearer 1500 c.c. This was a staggering blow at the time, but since then new "reconstructions" have been made with the result that the present capacity of the Piltdown cranium, according to its friends, is approximately 1300 c.c.. But even this figure is much too large to serve the purpose of the transformists.

To add to our confusion, Professors Gregory and Miller pointed out that the tooth described and used as the right lower canine, was no lower tooth of any kind at all, and not even a right tooth, but a left upper!

—37—

Prof. Ales Hrdlicka, leading American anthropologist, wrote in the Smithsonian Report for 1913, pp 491 552:

"A most important development in the study of the Piltdown remains is the recent well documented objection by Prof. Garrett S. Miller of the U. S. National Museum, to the classing together of the lower jaw, and the canine tooth with the cranium. According to Miller, who had ample anthropoid, as well as human material for comparison, the jaw and tooth belonged to a chimpanzee."

A. W. McCann, says of this:

"This is a heart-breaking admission; and even more heart breaking is the admission made by Hrdlicka himself when he urges that none of the conclusions regarding Piltdown man should be accepted, and that all hypotheses relating to it must be regarded as more or less premature."

Keith himself, in "The Antiquity of Man," p. 75, writes:

"The comparison of the fragments of the skull with corresponding parts of modern skulls, convinces students of anatomy that in general brain capacity, the head of the Piltdown race was remarkably similar to modern races."

And again on page 429, he affirms:

'Piltdown man saw, heard, thought, and dreamed much as we do."

It looks as if the scientists really did not know much at all about it! The reason for the uncertainty seems to be that the outlines of the Piltdown jaw are identical with those of a chimpanzee jaw. The molar teeth are identical with the ape form. The cranial fragments on the other hand, in practically all their details, are essentially human.

Prof. George Grant Mac Curdy of the Anthropological Department of Yale University, writing in "Science," Feb. 18, 1916, says:

> "Regarding the Piltdown specimens, we have at last reached a position that is tenable. The cranium is human as was recognized by all in the beginning. On the other hand, the mandible and the canine tooth belong to a chimpanzee."

Let Keith give the final judgment on this freak. He says in "The Antiquity of Man," p. 496:

> "We can say with certainty that the forehead of Eoanthropus was well formed. It was high, prominent, and, in width, equal to that of a modern skull."

And, on page 428, he gives the conclusion which would seem to invalidate all the claims made for "Eoanthropus."

> "We have in the Piltdown specimens, a certain assurance that one race of mankind had, so far as the mass of brain is concerned, a modern human standard, at the beginning of the Pleistocene period."

Then, if the Piltdown skull contained a brain of from 1300 c.c. to 1500 c.c. capacity, if the owner of this brain saw, felt, heard and dreamed much as we still do; was possessed of a high, prominent, well-formed forehead, surely we may ask where are the ape like characteristics which are certainly and badly needed if it is to offer any support to the theory of evolution.

Keith does not refer to the others in the well known series of alleged 'links' so it may be presumed that he does not have very much confidence himself in them.

HORMONES

The question of hormones as a possible cause of evolution, may be dismissed in a few words. The organs and tissues which produce these remarkable, mysterious, and little understood substances, used to be called "vestigial" and useless by the followers of Darwin. Now they are known to be indispensable to life. This is another instance of a discarded hypothesis, a great number of which strew the pathway of science.

Certainly we are safe in saying that there is nothing known about them which would lead us to believe that they can so change life forms that new species would eventually be produced.

The hope is obviously inspired by the sincere desire to discover some means by which evolution could be made to work. Hitherto, the 'factors' of evolution have eluded the most intense search. To one whose "brains are not scrambled" it would appear that the "fact" of evolution is just as strong, but no stronger than the "factors" of it.

CHANGE OF SPECIES

There is one statement which cannot be contradicted in this discussion and that is that evolution depends on numerous changes of species. Almost unlimited variation is admitted, but unless the types of life are definitely changed, transformism is absolutely impossible.

TRANSMISSION OF ACQUIRED CHARACTER

Also it is true, that these necessary changes of species cannot be brought about unless acquired characters are transmitted from one generation to another

What is the consensus of scientific opinion on these two vital points? J. Arthur Thomson, the Aberdeen

—40—

professor of Natural History, has already been quoted in regard to the Lamarckian theory of the transmission of acquired characteristics. He says that the idea is largely discarded for lack of evidence.

Professor Vernon Kellogg writes in 'Darwinism Today,' p. 4, as follows:

> "Mutations seem to be too few and far between; for orthogenesis we can discover no satisfactory mechanism; and the same is true for the Lamarckian theories of modification by the cumulation, through inheritance, of acquired or ontogenic characters. "Kurz und gut," we are immensely unsettled."

And, on page 18 of the same book, he says:

> "Speaking by and large, we only tell the general truth when we declare that no indubitable cases of species forming, that is, of descent, have been observed; and that no recognized case of natural selection really selecting has been observed."

Here are two momentous and fatal confessions, which ought, if true, forever to demolish faith in this imaginary concept.

Listen to Dr. David Starr Jordan of Stanford University, in "Science," October 20, 1922, p. 448:

> "None of the created 'new species' of plant or animal I know of would last five years in the open; nor is there the slightest evidence that any 'new species' of field or forest or ocean, ever originated from mutation, discontinuous variation or hybridization."

George Barry O'Toole writes on page 28, "The Case Against Evolution,":

> "Anyone thoroughly acquainted with the re-

sults of genetical analysis and research, will find it impossible to escape the conviction that there is no such thing as experimental evidence for evolution. In spite of the enormous advances made in the fields of genetics and cytology, the problem of the origin of species is, scientifically speaking, as mysterious as ever. No variation of which we have experience is interpretable as the transmutation of a specific type."

More, in "The Dogma of Evolution," p. 121, says:

"With all our contriving, we have never been able to produce a new species, and reversion to the common type occurs when indiscriminate breeding takes place."

Sir J. W. Dawson, in "The Origin of the World," p. 227, writes:

"No case is certainly known in human experience where any species of animal or plant has been so changed as to assume all the characters of a new species."

MUTATIONS

Mutation, or the occurrence of sudden large changes in a single generation, has been claimed to be the cause of new and distinct species and as the method by which perhaps evolution has occurred.

On this phase, we shall hear what Kellogg has to say in "Darminism To-Day, p. 19:

"We can only tell the general truth when we declare that no indubitable cases of species forming or transforming, that is, of descent, have been observed. I hasten to repeat the names of the Ancon sheep, the Paraguay cattle, the Porto Santo rabbit, the Artemis of Schmankewitch, and the De Vriesian Evening Primrose, to show that I know my list of classic possible exceptions to this denial of observed species forming, and to refer to Weldon's broad and narrow fronted crabs as a case of what may be an observation of selection at work. But such a list, if it could be extended to a score, or to a hundred, of cases, is **ludicrous** as objective proof of that descent and selection under whose domination, the forming of millions of species is **supposed** to have occurred."

Are these unequivocal statements anything less than a deathblow to evolution, delivered by one of its own advocates? Since this interesting phenomenon is so frequently used as evidence for the theory, one or two crushing deliverances are in order.

Prof. August Weismann, writes in "Darwin and Modern Science," pp. 23-24:

"Even if saltatory (sudden, large) variations do occur, we cannot assume that these have ever led to forms which are capable of survival under the conditions of wild life. Experience has shown that in plants which have suddenly varied, the power of persistence is diminished.

"It now appears that the far reaching conclusions drawn by De Vries from his observations on the Evening Primrose, rest upon a very insecure foundation. The plant from which De Vries saw 'numerous species'--his 'mutations' arise, was not, as he assumed, a wild species that had been introduced to Europe from America, but was probably a hybrid form which was first discovered in the Jardin des Plants in Paris, and which does not appear to exist anywhere in America as a wild species.

"This gives a severe shock to the 'Mutation

—43—

Theory,' for the other **actually** wild species with which De Vries experimented showed no 'mutations' but yielded negative results."

If this is not sufficient to send this 'factor' to oblivion forever, hear what Dr. Alfred Russell Wallace said in an article, "The Present Status of Darwinism," in the Contemporary Review, August, 1908:

"There is no proof whatever that in a state of nature such mutations are produced, except perhaps, very rarely; while the assumption that they have been and are produced so frequently as to constitute the mode by which ALL existing species have come into existence is a most illogical conclusion to draw from the phenomens presented by **one** species of plant of totally unknown parentage.

"These positive assertions as to what has occurred throughout the whole realm of organic nature in the whole course of its development, rest wholly on experiments with one plant, although these experiments are rendered comparatively valueless owing it its not being itself a wild species, but probably a hybrid. Was there ever such a mountain of theory reared upon such an almost infinitesimal basis of fact?"

This is strong language from a great man. Will the evolutionists listen to him and the others?

MENDELISM

Mendelism too, offers no hope to the ardent believer in a brute ancestry. Prof. W. B. Scott writes on this in "The Theory of Evolution," p. 163:

"Interesting and profoundly important as are the results of the Mendelian investigation....they have rendered but little assistance in making the evolutionary processes more intelligible, and instead of removing difficulties, they have rather increased them."

As if there were not enough difficulties before!

GEOLOGY

In order to complete this study of the present status of the entire evolutionary scheme, a few authoritative expressions of opinion concerning the geological evidence may be given, although Keith makes no mention of this phase. Many people believe that the evidence from the rocks is irrefutably in favor of evolution. Let us see.

Prof. A. C. Seward, Cambridge, in "Nature," April 26, 1924, writes:

"A student who takes an impartial retrospect, soon discovers that the fossil record raises more problems than it solves."

Herbert Spencer, in "Illustrations of Universal Progress," p. 376, said:

"The facts of palaeontology can never suffice either to prove or disprove the developmental hypothesis."

Dr. H. A. Nicholson, in "A Manual of Geology," p. 94, affirms:

"The geological record of the earth begins, indeed, with well developed representatives, of all the chief groups of the animal kingdom with the exception of the back-boned animals."

Prof. L. T. More, in "The Dogma of Evolution," says, p. 160:

"The more one studies palaeontology, the more

—45—

certain one becomes that evolution is based on faith alone."

In order to tell us how long and when the various forms of life existed on earth, geology gives definite names and time values to the different layers of strata. More's conclusion on this is found on page 151:

> "We can be certain that geology cannot, and never will be able to, translate the thickness of any stratum into an equivalent length of time, and that it cannot and never will be able to, establish real contemporaneousness of time in different parts of the world.

If this statement be true, then geology fails to support evolution.

O'Toole sums up a powerful argument against the evolutionary interpretation of geology in "The Case Against Evolution," p. 126:

> "Yet, what could be more enigmatic than the rock record as it stands?...The palaeontological argument is simply a theoretical construction which presupposes evolution instead of proving it. Its classic pedigrees of the horse, the camel, and the elephant, are only credible when we have assumed the 'fact' of evolution, and even then, solely upon condition that they claim to approximate, rather than assign, the actual ancestry of the animals in question."

> "In palaeontology, as in the field of zoology, evolution is not a conclusion but an interpretation. In palaeontology, otherwise than in the field of genetics, evolution is not amenable to the check of experimental tests, because here it deals not with that which **is**, but that which **was**....These obscure and fragmentary vestiges

of a vanished past, by reason of their very incompleteness, render themselves quite readily to all sorts of theories and all kinds of speculation."

WAR AMONG THE EVOLUTIONISTS

Accepting the conclusions of Darwin, who affirmed in "The Descent of Man," chapter six, p. 221, that man has come from the Old World Monkey, Keith is bound to believe in an ape ancestry for mankind.

A battle royal is on between the evolutionists themselves at the present time, and those sensible folks who repudiate the absurd claims of their opponents, are pleased to observe this violent internal warfare.

Maynard Shipley, in a recent article which he calls "Demonking Evolution-Osborn's Flirtation With the Shade of Bryan," gives us some interesting inside information.

> "The Fundamentalists have just gained new support for their crusade against the ape-man theory, and from no less an anti-Fundamentalist than "the Nestor of American palaeontologists," Dr. Henry Fairfield Osborn, Director of the American Museum of Natural History. Dr. Osborn....now concedes in effect, that, "so far as the descent of man from an ape ancestor is concerned, the learned Rev. John Roach Straton, and the still more erudite and now lamented William Jennings Byran, uttered but the truth in declaring that there are no fossil exhibits in the great museum of New York which demonstrate man's descent from some ancient anthropoid ancestor.... Dr. Osborn now regards **"the ape-man theory as totally false and misleading."**

Osborn, revoking his formed confident fiats, now

—47—

declares that we are not descended from an ape-like ancestor of Miocene Time, but from a distant stock (of the Oligocene period), which is assumed to have existed at that time. But, unfortunately, there are absolutely no fossil records of these very imaginary creatures. We are in a serious dilemma! Shall we believe Darwin and Keith, or shall we give our support to the more modern school headed by the "Nestor of American palaeontology?"

Shipley, manifesting a very seriously disturbed disposition, goes on to tell us that Osborn's opinion is that

> "Man sprang from a stock neither human nor ape-like but possessing certain common attributes which have been transmitted over this very long period of time (given as 16,000,000 years) to variously branching races of human beings who never passed through the simian stage on the one hand, and to variously branching races of anthropoid apes on the other."

We shall allow these authorities (?) to fight this out among themselves, with the probability that when the smoke of conflict has cleared away, nothing of either will be left to tell the tale. The truth is that all of them are wandering in an impenetrable fog of uncertainty, ignorance and credulity. No sooner is one theory opposed to creation, propounded, than it is demolished by someone of equal authority (?), with the result that every new concept is more grotesque than those which preceded!

THE BIBLE TRUE

The believer in the Biblical account of Creation occupies an impregnable and happy position. The Bible is scornfully indifferent to hatred, ridicule and bitter assault. Its age-long statements are never compelled to change because they are Infallible Truth. Every discovery in every realm of scientific investigation, substantiates, down to the minutest detail, the Scriptural Record.

The most potent and effective weapon which is being used by Satan in his present furious attack on the Bible, is evolution. He seems to have reserved this implement of war, for the closing days of this dispensation, soon to usher in the Millenial age when Satan will be overthrown and Truth will be triumphant, under the leadership of the coming King.

In this third decade of the twentieth century, no one need make any apology for accepting the Bible at its face value, and rejecting evolution with all other man-made explanations of the universe, based on false, God-eliminating ideas. The doctrine of evolution is utterly opposed to common-sense, science and Scripture, and has nothing to account for its existence except the purpose of some of its leading exponents to use it to prove the Word of God false and of human origin.

But, a Book written with such sustained dignity and meticulous precision, abounding in lightning-like phrases, arrows shot from the quiver of Infallible Wisdom, exhibiting the supernatural prescience of prophecy, contemptuously indifferent to the flippant insolence of a decadent skepticism, miraculously anticipating by thirty centuries the most stupendous discoveries of modern times, is not a patchwork of grotesque stupidity, incorporating a thousand mangled delusions, a monstrous travesty of Truth.

Such a Book is and must be the sublime embodiment of Omniscience, the supreme Gift to man from the Ruler and Creator of the Universe.

This remarkable Record is supreme in its history, its science, its ethics, and its spiritual concepts, every page revealing the imprint of the finger of God, and the divine illumination of Deity.

Therefore when Darwin or Keith tells us that evolution is true, and the Bible false, we reply, "No," and reiterate our unshakeable faith in the sublime statement of God Himself,—"In the beginning, God created."

ACKNOWLEDGMENTS

Brown, Arthur I. *Evolution and the Bible.* (1920s): 1–32. Courtesy of Ronald L. Numbers.

Brown, Arthur I. *Evolution and the Blood-Precipitation Test.* (1920s): 1–31. Courtesy of Wheaton College.

Brown, Arthur I. *God's Creative Forethought.* (1920s): 1–35. Courtesy of Wheaton College.

Brown, Arthur I. *Men, Monkeys and Missing Links.* (1923): 1–31. Courtesy of Ronald L. Numbers.

Brown, Arthur I. *Science Speaks to Osborn.* (1927): 1–30. Courtesy of Calvin College and Seminary Library.

Brown, Arthur I. *Was Darwin Right?* (c.1927): 1–50. Courtesy of Ronald L. Numbers.

For Product Safety Concerns and Information please contact our EU representative GPSR@taylorandfrancis.com
Taylor & Francis Verlag GmbH, Kaufingerstraße 24, 80331 München, Germany

www.ingramcontent.com/pod-product-compliance
Lightning Source LLC
Chambersburg PA
CBHW062222300426
44115CB00012BA/2175